CDL Exam Prep 2020-2021

A CDL Study Guide with 425 Test Questions and Answer Explanations for the Commercial Driver's License Exam (Training Book for All Classes)

Table of Contents

Background Information

The United States first began licensing drivers in 1901 in New York City as a regulatory move designed to ensure that only credible and qualified drivers were on the road. This was a result of the increasing number of vehicles on American roads.

Although in 1903 Missouri and Massachusetts became the first states to officially require a driver's license, drivers were not required to pass a test and licenses were issued to any driver who applied.

In 1919, Rhode Island became the first state to require both vehicle registration and a driver's license.

Eventually, all vehicle owners began to be asked to register their vehicles. Failure to register or obtain a license could result in a driving ban for a person.

By 1935, 39 states required driver's licenses but only a handful required a test before issuing them. This was in spite of the increasing rate of driving-related issues among incompetent drivers across the country.

Today, the entire country requires all vehicle owners to register their vehicles. Drivers are also required to be licensed by their state of residence before getting behind a wheel.

Another change in United States driving regulations occurred on October 27, 1986. Before then, anyone could drive a commercial vehicle in the US, with or without a Commercial Driver's License (CDL). On that day, the government signed the Commercial Motor Vehicle Safety Act (CMVSA) into law requiring every commercial driver in the country to have a CDL. This requires US-based large truck operators and drivers to undergo rigorous training to qualify for the license. The CMVSA has had a tremendous effect on highway safety over the years.

What is a Commercial Driver's License?

In the United States, a Commercial Driver's License, as the name implies, is a type of license that is required to drive tractor trailers, passenger buses and other vehicles that are classified as commercial motor vehicles (CMVs).

Types of CDL Licenses

As a commercial motor vehicle driver, you can apply for any of the three different classes of licenses issued by your state. These are:

1. **Class A**

A driver who wishes to drive two or more vehicles that have a combined weight of 26,001 pounds or more can apply for this license class. However, the driver should note that the towed vehicle should weigh over 10,000 pounds while the second vehicle will make up for the remaining weight.

If you have a Class A license, you can drive a wide range of vehicles that includes tank vehicles, tractor-trailers, livestock carriers, trailer and truck combinations and flatbeds. Note that if you have the right endorsement with your CDL Class A license, you may be allowed to drive some Class B or Class C vehicles.

There are five types of endorsements. Each endorsement allows you to drive a specific vehicle. These are:

- **H Endorsement**

With this endorsement you can drive a vehicle that is used in transporting hazardous materials. The material must be clearly labeled per state and federal regulations. You must pass both the Hazmat Knowledge Test and the Transportation Safety Administration (TSA) Background Check before you can apply for the endorsement.

- **N Endorsement**

This endorsement allows you to drive a commercial vehicle such as a tank for transporting liquid. The tank must be either temporarily or permanently attached to the chassis or the vehicle. Passing the Tank Knowledge Test is a requirement for this endorsement.

- **P Endorsement**

If you have this endorsement, you are eligible to drive a vehicle that carries at least 16 passengers. You must pass the Passenger Transport Road Skills Test and the Passenger Transport Knowledge Test to qualify for this endorsement.

- **S Endorsement**

The S endorsement is for individuals who wish to drive a school bus with a minimum capacity of 16 passengers. Applicants for the S endorsement must pass both the School Bus Road Skills Test and the School Bus Knowledge Test. Some states, such as New Hampshire, require applicants to have a School Bus Certificate before they are issued the S endorsement.

- **T Endorsement**

The endorsement allows you to drive either a double or triple trailer. You must pass the Doubles/Triples Knowledge Test to qualify for this endorsement. Note that New Hampshire doesn't allow drivers to operate triple trailers in the state, regardless of endorsement.

2. **Class B**

You can only drive a single vehicle with this class of license. The gross combination weight of the vehicle must be 26,001 pounds or more. You can also tow a vehicle that weighs less than 10,000 pounds.

This class of license is ideal for driving large passenger buses, box trucks, straight trucks, tractor-trailers, segmented buses and dump trucks that have small trailers attached. A Class B license is also required for delivery trucks, tow trucks and garbage trucks. If you have the right endorsement, you can drive some Class C vehicles with this license.

3. **Class C**

You need this license if you wish to transport a minimum of 16 passengers, including the driver. It is also the recommended license for people who want to transport materials that federal law classifies as hazardous (hazmat).

Thus, as a Class C license holder, you are licensed to drive passenger vans, small hazmat vehicles and other combination vehicles that are not included in the other classes.

These are the types of CDL licenses available. Choose the license that meets your needs and work towards getting the appropriate endorsement. Once you meet the requirements, you will be licensed as soon as possible.

Introduction

Having a driver's license may open the door to various driving opportunities for you. The first step towards becoming a commercial driver is having a government-approved license. This is proof of your eligibility to handle a specific type of vehicle and ensures the safety of other road users, including pedestrians.

This guide provides insight into how you can pass the Commercial Driver's License Exam. It discusses the major areas that people are generally tested upon. Hence, the book is divided into sections that are designed to test your driving knowledge in different areas such as hazmat and air brakes. Your theoretical and practical driving knowledge of passenger or tanker transport and other types of vehicles will be tested too.

Additionally, this guide provides valuable information such as the exam date, dos and don'ts on exam day and proven test-taking tips that will help you to pass the exam with flying colors.

To assist you with your preparation for the exam, the book contains 450 multiple-choice questions drawn from the various aspects of driving that the test will cover. The questions will test your knowledge of the information in the book. The more time you spend on these exams honing your skills, the better you will do.

At the end of each practice test, you will find answers to the questions along with a short explanation.

Reread the information in this guide as needed and retake the practice tests until you're confident.

General Section

In this section, you will learn the exam rules, format and how to register for the exam and take it.

Test Format

The CDL exam is divided into eight sections:

1. General Knowledge
2. Air Brakes
3. Hazmat
4. Combination Vehicles
5. Tanker
6. Doubles and Triples
7. Passenger Transport
8. School Bus.

Prospective drivers are required to answer 50 multiple-choice questions divided among those eight sections. To pass the test you have to get at least an 80%, meaning at least 40 out of 50 questions right.

You have 60 minutes to take the test. Thus, it's critical that you prepare carefully. That's what this book is designed to help you do.

Test Rules

The test rules include details about what applicants are expected to bring to the test center as well as dos and don'ts of the exam.

Candidates should bring the following to the exam center:

- **Proof of identity:** You are required to present proof of identity at the examination center. This could be a birth certificate or a commercial learner's permit.

  Otherwise, a government-issued ID, U.S. military discharge papers or valid military ID is acceptable. Note that photocopies of documents are not permitted. Documents must be original.

- **Proof of citizenship or permanent residency:** This may include a birth certificate, US passport, permanent residency card or certificate of citizenship. You can also present your voter registration card, payroll check or check stub. Other acceptable documents for proof of residency are a state income tax return or IRS W-2 form. Your full name and address must appear on the document in the same order and format as on your license application form.

- **Proof of social security number:** The following documents are accepted as proof of a valid social security number: check stub or payroll check, social security card, valid U. S. military identification card or your income tax return for the preceding year.

Eligibility Requirements

Aside from the documents detailed above, you must meet some other basic requirements before you are allowed to take the test.

These requirements include:

- You must have a commercial learner's permit (CLP). This permit is issued by a state to authorize holders to test their skills in operating commercial motor vehicles. Obtaining this permit is the first requirement for all prospective commercial driver's license applicants. It is recommended that you have the CLP for a minimum of 14 days before applying to take the test.
- Though most states issue this permit for applicants aged 21 and above, applicants between ages 18 and 20 are allowed to apply. Such drivers, however, are only allowed to operate within their state of legal residence. If you have this intrastate permit, your state will automatically remove the restrictions once you are 21.
- If you are considering driving a commercial vehicle, it is imperative that you pass the general knowledge exam and other exams that are specific to the type of vehicle you wish to drive. For instance, if you want to operate a school bus, in addition to the general knowledge exam, you must also take the passenger vehicle and school bus exams.
- You must possess a non-commercial driver's license. This is proof of your driving knowledge and experience and is necessary to show that you can handle commercial vehicles.
- For intrastate driving, you must be 18 years or older.
- You must be at least 21 years old for interstate driving. This is also the age requirement for transporting hazardous materials.
- You must be able to speak and read English fluently. This is because drivers are expected to be able to easily read and understand driving regulations, road signs, etc.
- A disqualified driver is not eligible to take the test. The disqualification applies to all forms of driving, including commercial driving.
- Physical and mental fitness is a must. Drivers who wish to operate commercial motor vehicles must have 20/40 vision in each eye. For horizontal vision, 140 degrees or higher is considered acceptable.

You are expected to meet each of these visual requirements without glasses or contacts. This is to ensure that you can see potential causes of accidents and avoid them. You also need to be able to hear other road users.

Finally, your blood pressure and sugar levels must be within what is considered a medically acceptable range.

Do *not* take the following to the exam center:

- Study aids such as written materials or notes.
- Any form of electronic devices such as iPads or cell phones.
- Personal effects.

If you are caught breaking any of these rules, you will not be allowed to take the test or to gain your CDL.

Conditions for Disqualifications

It's possible to be banned from driving a commercial vehicle for at least a year if you are found guilty of the following offenses:

- Driving under the influence of drugs or alcohol. Alcohol and drugs can impair your sight and reflexes. This makes you more vulnerable to crashes that may injure you and other road users.
- Your blood alcohol content (BAC) is 0.04 or higher while driving a commercial vehicle. This can lead to a 60-day license suspension or could even be a lifetime ban. Note that the disqualification is limited to commercial vehicles only.
- Refusing to take a breath or blood test while driving a commercial vehicle. This incurs the same penalty as testing with a high BAC.
- Committing a felony with a commercial motor vehicle.
- Lying on your license application form.
- Failing to stop at an accident scene that involves your vehicle, especially if the accident leads to a loss of life or injury.

If you commit any of the above offenses while transporting hazardous materials, your license will be revoked for three years.

Under some conditions, a driver may receive a lifetime disqualification. These conditions include:

- Being found guilty of manufacturing or distributing drugs illegally with a commercial motor vehicle.
- Being convicted twice of one of the violations listed above.

You may also receive different degrees of restrictions depending on your offense. You can contact the local CDL office for a comprehensive list of offenses and the degree of penalties attached to them.

Taking the Test

Visit your local Department of Motor Vehicles' (DMV) official website to choose a time to take the test and pay the necessary fees.

Most DMVs conduct road tests on business days only (i.e., not on weekends or federal holidays).

Make sure you arrive at the test center at least 30 minutes before the test time. If you arrive at the venue late, you will be required to reschedule the test. This can be problematic if you urgently need to pass the exam.

How to Register for the Exam

To register for the exam, simply visit the corresponding website for your state of residence. The local DMV office will provide you with information about the registration process.

Where to Take the Test

You can take the test in any accredited center. When you visit the official DMV website for your state, you will see a list of approved test centers. Choose any of the sites that is convenient for you, considering distance and any other applicable factors.

How Often Can You Take the Test?

With each permit, you are allowed to take the test a maximum of three times. The interval between two tests is determined by the applicant's age. If you are above 18 years and fail the test, you are required to wait for at least a day before attempting the test again.

Applicants who are below 18 and fail the test must wait for a minimum of seven days before they can take the examination again. The interval is designed to allow you to review for the exam once more. Take the opportunity to practice more for the test and improve your driving skills.

Note that you are permitted to renew your permit for as long as you are physically fit to operate a vehicle.

How to Reschedule the Test

If you must reschedule your test for any reason such as road construction, bad weather, change of job, etc. you are required to cancel your first appointment. Then, select a new date. Be aware that it is illegal to schedule more than one test appointment simultaneously.

The following conditions may cause the test to be rescheduled:

- The examiner won't risk conducting the test in inclement weather such as snow or poor visibility.
- If you or your vehicle don't meet the road test requirements.
- Other circumstances beyond the DMV's control that may make it difficult to proceed with the test.

What Students Can and Cannot Do

While taking the test make sure you always:

- Wear your seat belt.
- Come to a stop at stop signs and red lights.
- Keep your cool.

Also ensure that you do *not:*

- Run a red light.
- Panic under pressure.
- Cut corners when driving winding roads.
- Drive on curbs.

As much as possible, make sure you avoid accidents. Follow the advice this guide provides to ensure you aren't disqualified from taking the exam.

Additional Tips for Obtaining the License

- **Avoid drugs:** If you plan to take the CDL test, it is imperative that you don't do drugs. Drivers are subjected to random drug tests and failing a drug test is one way you can be disqualified.
- **Prepare for the exam:** This isn't a hugely difficult test. As long as you carefully prepare by reading this guide, taking the practice tests and practicing your driving skills, you should do well.

- **Keep calm:** Some drivers fail the test simply because they don't do well under pressure. Your ability to keep your cool in the face of difficulties and pressure will make a huge difference between failing and passing the test.

Tips for Passing the Test

- Get enough rest the night before the test. Insufficient rest will make you feel tired, sleepy and will impact your concentration during the test. A lack of concentration, triggered by tiredness, makes you more prone to accidents. You can imagine the outcome if you suddenly become sleepy behind the wheel.
- Read each question over again before answering. This is a test of your theoretical and practical driving knowledge. Although the questions are not difficult if you prepare well for the exam, if you don't understand a question, you could make a mistake in your answer choice. Be aware of the time limit but also don't rush.
- Listen to any oral or written instructions. Failure to do so may cause your disqualification.
- Take a short rest when you are stressed. Yes, you do have a time limit, but taking a moment or two to calm yourself is important.
- Don't drink caffeine shortly before taking the test. Caffeine can impact your focus, so avoid it up to eight hours before the exam.
- Don't bring your cell phone into the exam center. If the phone rings while taking the test, you will be penalized and disqualified.
- If you are sure of your answer, don't second guess yourself. Go with your first instinct.
- Be optimistic when preparing for the test. A positive mindset yields a positive outcome.
- Practice! Practice!! Practice!!! Devote enough time to practicing for the test. You can take advantage of available resources, such as this guide, to equip yourself for success.

CDL Road Skills Test

Apart from the written test, the CDL exam also includes a road skills tests. Before you are deemed eligible for this part of the test, you must meet the following requirements:

- Have a valid learner's permit for a minimum of 30 days.
- Schedule an appointment online for the test through the state's DMV.

On test day:

- Go to the Commercial Driver Road Test Lot.
- Arrive at the test venue at least 15 minutes before the test.
- Make sure that the vehicle you drive to the test fulfills the requirements for the particular vehicle you intend to drive.
- The vehicle must be duly registered with proof of insurance.
- Have a valid learner's permit. You won't be allowed to take the test without the permit. Remember, the permit is also a prerequisite for obtaining the driver's license.
- If you are under 21, make sure you take your 40-hour Certification of Eligibility for Provisional License form.
- Wear your seat belt. All drivers, irrespective of the vehicle they operate, are mandated by the government to always wear a seat belt.

It is considered illegal to drive yourself to the venue unaccompanied by a licensed driver. Aside from having the road skills test appointment canceled on the spot, you won't be allowed to take the test for another six months.

Tips for Passing the Road Test

When you are preparing for the road test, bear the following in mind:

1. Lack of adequate preparation is one of the leading causes of failure for most new drivers. According to the DMV, you should have at least 50 hours of supervised driving practice under your belt before taking the exam. The more you practice, the better the chances of a successful test outcome.

2. Spend at least 15 hours practicing driving at sunset, to get used to night driving. This is a necessity if your job description requires driving at night or if you're going to be on the highways at night.

3. You should also devote 10 hours to practicing in both moderate and heavy traffic.

4. Pay attention to how you brake. You should always stop the vehicle gently. To avoid a jerky stop, start braking before you reach the stopping position. If you are asked to stop the vehicle in a lane, make sure that you park in the proper position. This counts a lot during a road skills test. If you can't apply the brakes properly, you will lose valuable points.

5. How you switch gears can have a huge impact on your performance. To start with, make sure your vehicle is always in the correct gear. This is irrespective of your vehicle's transmission system: manual or automatic. When it is time to shift

gears, do so smoothly. If you grind the gear while switching it, your examiner will take notice.

6. Don't drive too close to the vehicle you are following. Always leave enough space to avoid an accident if anything happens to the vehicle in front of you. For example, a heavy vehicle in front of you may not be able to ascend a mountain road properly. There are cases where such vehicles descend roads uncontrollably. If you are close to them, accidents become inevitable. But if you keep a reasonable distance between you and the vehicle in front of you, you can easily get out of harm's way and prevent such accidents.

7. If you are driving in bad weather or poor visibility, keep as much distance as possible between you and the vehicle in front.

8. Your examiner may ask you to stop while driving. Make sure that you don't stop at an intersection but before it. Also, stop the vehicle before you reach crosswalks or stop lines.

   If you are obstructed after parking behind a crosswalk, leave the spot until you have a clear view of the front. Always ensure you are not obstructed wherever you park.

9. Observe your environment. Look for potential problems and hazards and avoid them. Consistently check your mirrors. You can easily avoid running into another vehicle if you stay alert.

   When changing lanes, it is advisable to look at your mirrors. Complement that by looking over your shoulders from time to time too. This enables you to back up or change lanes safely.

10. Obey speed limits. When driving, look out for posted speed limits and abide by them. However, while paying attention to speed limits, consider other factors such as visibility or weather. If the weather or visibility is bad, drive at a lower speed. Safe driving should be paramount to you, not driving at a specific speed.

11. You are not the only road user. You can only predict your driving and not that of others. Nevertheless, you can drive safely by anticipating other drivers' driving.

12. Make sure you understand road signals and signs. Pavement markings convey important information to road users. They help you to know the parts of the road you can use as well as provide useful information about the condition of the road

ahead. The markings also enable drivers to know where they are and are not allowed to pass.

Yellow lines on the pavement are used to separate traffic that is flowing in opposite directions and prevent vehicles from running into each other. For instance, a solid yellow line indicates that a portion of the road is closed to the public. However, you can use areas that are marked with yellow dashes.

13. Communication is crucial to safe driving. While driving, communicate effectively with other road users, both pedestrians and drivers. Hook your horn when necessary, especially to warn absentminded road users of your presence. You can also warn reckless drivers to be more cautious.

14. Trafficators (more commonly known as blinkers) are also important. Using your blinkers appropriately is a preventive measure against collisions. Once other drivers have a clear idea of where you want to turn, they will avoid using that path.

The examiner will assess several factors during the test. When you make a driving mistake, points will be deducted. To pass the test, the points deducted must not be more than 30.

If you are involved in an accident or violate traffic laws during the test, you will be automatically disqualified.

If you fail the CDL road test, you have a chance to further practice your driving skills and retake the test for $40.

General Restrictions Types

Based on their particular license, drivers are prohibited from operating some types of Commercial Motor Vehicles.

The common restrictions, aside from state-based restrictions, are:

1. **B Restriction**

This type of restriction requires a driver to use corrective lenses while operating a commercial motor vehicle.

2. **C Restriction**

If you need a mechanical aid to drive a commercial motor vehicle, this restriction will be noted on your driver's license or learner's permit.

3. D Restriction

This restriction means you can only operate a commercial vehicle with a prosthetic aid.

4. E Restriction

This restriction means you can't operate a commercial vehicle with a manual transmission if during the skills test you used a vehicle with an automatic or semiautomatic transmission. The local DMV can remove this restriction on two conditions:

- If you hold a CLP without a restriction for two weeks.
- If you pass a road skills test in a commercial motor vehicle that doesn't have an automatic transmission.

5. G Restriction

The DMV may restrict some drivers to driving in daylight only. If you have a G restriction on your license and are caught driving at night, you may be subject to penalties.

6. L Restriction

This restriction on your license or permit implies that you are not qualified to drive a commercial motor vehicle with air brakes if you:

- Took your road test with a vehicle that didn't have air brakes.
- Didn't check the air brake system properly.
- Couldn't identify the air brake system components properly.
- Didn't pass the air brakes knowledge test.

The L Restriction can be removed by the DMV if:

- You hold a learner's permit that doesn't have the restriction for 14 days.
- You pass the required skills test in a Class A vehicle.

7. M Restriction

Having this restriction code on your CDL or CLP means that you are forbidden from operating a Class A passenger vehicle or school bus if your skills test for this special endorsement was done with a Class B passenger vehicle. However, you can operate a Class B or a Class C school bus or passenger vehicle in spite of the restriction.

Hence, if you have a Class A driver's license but obtain your school bus endorsement (S) or passenger endorsement (P) in a Class B vehicle, this restriction will be placed on your license.

If you want the restrictions removed, the DMV will do so provided that:

- You hold a restriction-free CLP for 14 days.
- You pass the skills test in the right Class A passenger vehicle.

8. N Restriction

If you have a Code N restriction on your CDL or CLP, you can't operate a Class A or Class B passenger vehicle. Hence, your school bus endorsement or passenger endorsement in a Class B vehicle automatically forbids you from driving other classes of vehicles except the Class C vehicle if that is what you used to obtain your passenger endorsement.

The local DMV office can overrule the restriction if:

- You hold a CLP without restrictions for at least 14 days.
- You pass the skills test with a Class A or Class B passenger vehicle.

9. O Restriction

The O restriction forbids drivers from operating commercial motor vehicle tractors of any sort. Thus, if this appears on your commercial learner's permit or commercial driver's license, a tractor with a fifth-wheel connection is off the list of vehicles you can operate. This is especially true if you don't use a fifth-wheel connection on your vehicle while attempting the skills test but used a pintle hook, ball, goose neck or chain hookup.

The local DMV office can overrule the restriction if:

- You pass the skills test.
- You hold a learner's permit that doesn't have the restriction for at least 14 days.

10. P Restriction

This restricts your scope of operation to commercial vehicles that exclude passenger-carrying Class A, B or C vehicles.

This restriction on your license or permit allows you to operate a passenger vehicle provided that the passengers are federal or state inspectors and auditors. Other people you can transport are test examiners, the CDL supervising driver or other trainees.

The local licensing office can overrule the restriction if:

- You pass any relevant knowledge test for the specific vehicle you are driving.
- You hold a permit without a Class P restriction for 14 days.
- You pass the skills test for the class of vehicle you want to drive.

11. P1 Restriction

This is a special type of P Restriction. Drivers who have this restriction code on their CDL or CLP can't operate a CMV besides the ones defined by the Federal Motor Carrier Safety Administration. More so, it is not mandatory to meet the requirements needed for the USDOT medical certificate.

However, the licensing department can waive the restriction under the following conditions:

- You present the DMV with a DOT medical certificate.
- You meet the DMV Form DL-405A, CDL Holders Medical Certification Requirements.

When selecting your type of vehicle, choose options other than the "Excepted Interstate" option.

12. V Restriction

This restriction is otherwise known as the Medical Variance restriction. Its presence on your learner's permit or driver's license implies that the government offers you a medical variance which is a skills performance evaluation or federal waiver alongside your DOT medical certification. Contained in the medical variance are some ailments such as hearing problems, diabetes, vision impairments and seizures.

For as long as your medical variance is referenced by the DOT medical certificate, the DMV won't lift this restriction.

13. X Restriction

Another name for this restriction is no cargo in a tank. This means that you may not drive commercial motor tank vehicles that have not been fully emptied.
Hence, if the tank has been previously used to transport hazardous substances or materials, it must be purged before you can drive it. As the operator, you are legally required to have a purge certificate.

14. Z Restriction

With this restriction you can't drive a commercial motor vehicle that uses air brakes. This is especially true if you did your test with a vehicle with air brakes instead of hydraulic brakes.

Air over hydraulic brakes use a combination of hydraulic brake principles and air brakes.

If you satisfy the conditions below, the DMV will waive the restriction:

- You pass all relevant examinations on the vehicle you wish to operate.
- You hold a learner's permit that doesn't carry a restriction for a minimum of 14 days.
- You pass both the on-road and vehicle inspection skills test.

We have reviewed general test-taking and licensing information in this chapter. Next, we will discuss the first of the test sections, Air Brakes.

Chapter One: Air Brakes

Air brakes are some of the most important parts of a commercial vehicle motor. An air brake is otherwise known as a compressed air brake system. It is classified as a friction brake and is commonly found in vehicles that use compressed air for braking, rather than hydraulic fluid. The compressed air presses on the piston, applying the brake to the brake pad. The brake pad is saddled with the primary responsibility of stopping the vehicle once the right amount of pressure is applied.

Air brakes are commonly used in buses, semitrailers, trucks and trailers. They were first developed by George Westinghouse to be used in railways. Their effectiveness in the railway system contributed to their increasing popularity. Over the years, they gradually found their way into commercial vehicles.

The primary advantage of using the air brake system is its reliability. You can imagine the deadly effect if a speeding vehicle using hydraulic brakes suddenly runs out of fluid because of an undetected leak. Using air brakes prevents such an unfortunate accident. Hence, drivers of commercial vehicles use air brakes to ensure this kind of accident does not occur.

In simple terms, air brake systems are the preferred braking systems in large commercial vehicles due to their ability to develop high mechanical forces and transmit them over great distances. This braking system depends on some connections and simple components including compressed air that is stored in tanks. The compressed air produces the force that is applied to each wheel to make the braking system effective.

When a driver presses the brake pedal, the compressed air is transported from one part of the braking system to another. This makes braking possible. Some special valves ensure that the air is transported swiftly so that the vehicle stops as soon as the brakes are applied.

Components of Air Brakes in Buses and Trucks

The most common air brake systems are foundation brakes. These are found in buses and trucks. This brake system adopts the triple-valve principle that is common in rail cars. If the pressure in the reservoir is lower than in the train, the triple valve will connect the train to the reservoir feed. The connection will increase the air pressure in the reservoir.

Thus, air gradually builds up in the air lines or brake pipes to release the brake. The triple valve can also cause the exhaustion of the brake cylinder and thus release the brakes in the process. This principle is also used in the braking system.

A graduated release system releases the brakes. When the pressure in the system increases partially, the brake will be released in proportion to the increased pressure. Conversely, if the pressure decreases, the brake will react accordingly.

Air brakes contain the following components:

- **Air Reservoir Tanks:** The brake system needs pressurized or compressed air to function. The air reservoir tanks hold enough air that the brakes can be used over and over again regardless of whether the compressor is working or not. Vehicles use different sizes and numbers of air reservoir tanks.
- **Push Rod:** This is a steel rod that shares some similarities with the piston connecting the slack adjuster and the brake chamber. When the rod is depressed, the brakes are immediately released. Extending the push rod automatically applies the brakes.
- **Air Compressor**: The air compressor is a very important component of the air brake. This compressor pumps the air which the brake system needs for operation into storage tanks in the system. It both builds and maintains the air pressure that is needed to operate the air brakes. The compressor performs the same function for other air-powered accessories in the vehicle.

  The air compressor connects to the engine through a v-belt or gears. This component may be air cooled or cooled through the engine cooling system. It may be lubricated by engine oil or by the engine in the compressor itself. Before you start driving, check the engine level, if the compressor comes with one.
- **Slack Adjuster**: An arm of the slack adjuster connects both the brake chamber and the push rod. This makes it possible to control the distance between the two brake shoes for easier and faster braking.
- **Brake Chambers**: The brake chamber is a cylindrical container. The slack adjuster that moves the cam mechanism or diaphragm is housed in the brake chamber
- **Air Compressor Governor**: The air compressor has a cut-out (125 psi) and cut-in (100 psi) point controlled by the air compressor governor. This ensures the air compressor has the required amount of air in the tanks. Hence, while the air compressor works continuously as long as the engine runs, the compressor controls and limits the air compression because it is tasked with the responsibility of loading and unloading the compressor.

  Air is usually pumped into the reservoirs when the compressor is loaded. When it is not loaded, the compressor pumps the needed air between the two cylinders. At that stage, it doesn't supply air to the reservoirs.

When the air pressure in the tank rises to the cut-out level, the governor stops it from pumping air. At the cut-in level, the governor allows it to pump air again.

- **Foot Valve**: Depressing the foot valve, otherwise known as the brake pedal, releases air from the reservoir tanks. When you remove the pressure by lifting your foot, the brake is disengaged and the air pressure is reduced.

  When you release the brakes, the system releases some air, reducing the air pressure in the tanks. The air compressor has the responsibility of replenishing the released air to ensure the brake works properly.

  Note that if you are fond of pressing and releasing the brake pedal for no apparent reason, the air in the brake system will be released at a faster rate than it can be replaced by the compressor. Thus, the compressor will run out of air faster, leaving insufficient air for the brake system to use.
- **Drain Valves**: The brake contains air tanks. These are used to drain air from a vehicle when it is not in use. You can release the valves in the tanks with the aid of the drain valves.
- **Brake Shoe**: The brake shoe is a lined steel mechanism that produces friction when in contact with the brake drum. As a part of the braking system, it uses friction to stop a moving vehicle when the brakes are applied.
- **Brake S-Cam**: This is an integral part of the braking system, commonly used in trucks and other heavy vehicles. This cam is shaped in the form of the letter "S." It performs two major functions. It separates the brakes by pushing them apart and also pushes them against the brake drum. The S-Cam is currently used in 85% of vehicles equipped with air brakes in the United States.
- **Return Spring**: The return spring is a stiff spring which is vital to the brake system. It's connected to the brake shoes and returns the shoes to the appropriate open position when the brakes are not spread by either the diaphragm or the S-Cam.
- **Safety Valve:** This valve is usually installed in the first tank that receives air from the compressor. It protects the tank and the entire brake system from excessive pressure that can damage it. By default, the safety valve doesn't release air. If it does for some reason, it needs to be fixed immediately.
- **Alcohol Evaporator**: Some air brake systems are designed with an alcohol evaporator. This comes in handy in colder climates. It reduces the risk of the air brake valves becoming iced over.

  You should check the alcohol container regularly. When necessary, fill it up. You may have to do this daily during cold weather to keep the brakes working.

To remove oil and water from the evaporator, you must drain the air tank daily, unless the tank comes with automatic drain valves.

- **Air Tank Drains:** Compressed air is usually contaminated with compressor oil and water. This will have a negative impact on the air brake system, causing it to malfunction.

  For instance, it is a common phenomenon for water to freeze in the tank during cold weather and cause the brake to fail. Oil and water may also settle at the bottom of the tank and cause a malfunction.

  Thus, it is imperative that you drain the air tank regularly using the drain valve at the bottom of each air tank.

  There are two types of drain valves. One is operated manually by pulling a cable or turning a quarter turn. After completing your activities for the day, drain the tanks. The automatic valve expels oil and water automatically. This makes it a lot easier to keep the tank dry. If you wish, you can equip the tanks with manual draining too.

  Automatic air tanks are also equipped with electric heating devices that prevent the contents of the air tank from freezing in cold weather.
- **Spring Brakes**: Truck tractors, trucks and buses are all equipped with parking and emergency brakes. These are held together by mechanical force to prevent accidental leakage of the air pressure. Spring brakes are used to provide the mechanical force that prevents the leakage.

  Air pressure holds power springs back while operating a heavy vehicle. The springs will apply the brakes if the air pressure is removed. The driver can release the air from the spring brakes with a parking brake control and allow the springs to apply the brake. If the air brake system leaks and causes the loss of air, it will still allow the springs to apply the brakes.

  Straight trucks and tractor have spring brakes too. The brakes are fully operational when the air pressure in the brake drops to between 20 and 30 psi. At that stage, it may not be advisable to wait until the brakes are automatically applied. As soon as you see the buzzer and the low air pressure warning light, stop the vehicle while the brake is still under control.

  While the spring brakes are powerful, their braking power is dependent on how the brakes are adjusted. In badly adjusted brakes, the regular brakes won't work. The parking/emergency brakes will malfunction as well.

- **Parking Brake Controls:** If you are driving a new heavy vehicle, chances are that it comes with air brakes. To operate the parking brakes, you will use a yellow push/pull control knob. Pulling the knob applies the brake and pushing it releases the brake. In older vehicles, a lever can be used to control the parking brake. It is recommended that you always apply the parking brake when you park a vehicle.

  A note of caution: when the spring brakes are on, don't push the brake pedal down. This is to prevent accidental damage to the pedal due to the heavy pressure from both the air pressure and the springs. While some vehicles are designed with a mechanism that prevents this from happening, remembering not to apply pressure on the brake pedal when the spring brakes are on is best.

How do Air Brakes Work?

When the vehicle is idle, the vehicle's air system will be charged as the brake is not depressed. Then, the air pressure in the brake system will overcome the S-Cam or the diaphragm in a closed position. This will result in the brake system being released. Once you depress the brake pedal, the pressure will decrease gradually. The decrease will turn the S-Cam while the brake shoes are simultaneously spread against the drum. This will cause the reservoir tanks to be filled by the compressor so that the air pressure increases again as the pedal retracts.

The emergency air brakes play a complementary role to the compressor, enhancing the performance of the air brake system. You can activate the emergency air brake by pulling the emergency air brake button on the dash.

It is mandatory that you push the emergency brake button to give the air brake system enough air before you drive a vehicle with the air brake system. The emergency brake will remain in a free state once the emergency system is pressurized.

Even if there is a leak in the system, the air pressure will still have sufficient pressure to engage the emergency brake.

Air brake systems are a combination of three braking systems:

1. **The Service Brake System**: This applies the brakes and releases them when you use the brake pedal while driving normally. This braking system is used for slow driving or when you want to stop. To apply it, push the brake pedal and route the air under pressure at approximately 100 to 120 psi (6.89 to 8.27 bar or 690 to 830 kpa) to the vehicle's brake chamber. This will engage the brake to slow the vehicle or stop it completely.
2. **The Parking Brake System**: This is a part of the air braking system that is engaged when you use the parking brake control.

The parking brake system contains a drum or disc designed in a way that spring pressure can keep it in the "applied" position.

3. **The Emergency Brake System**: This brake system, otherwise known as an e-brake or hand brake, stops the vehicle if there is a brake system failure. When this system is engaged, it releases the available pressurized air in the lines between the brakes and the compressed air storage tank. This immediately engages the parking brake.

Thus, you have a braking system that is designed to allow you to stop your vehicle whenever you want and prevent unfortunate accidents. Aside from its use during emergencies, it can also be used to keep vehicles motionless when parked.

It is noteworthy that the majority of truck air brakes are powered by drum brakes. However, the disc brake system is gradually gaining ground.

Most heavy vehicles have a built-in gauge that indicates whether there is enough air pressure in the brake system or not. You may get a warning light or hear a warning sound if the air pressure is way below the recommended level.

It is also common to see what is generally referred to as a wig wag. This device drops down automatically when the air pressure falls below the recommended level. It enables the driver to see the low level and act promptly.

Air brakes also come with a warning signal that goes off before the pressure in the air pressure tank falls below 60 psi. The red warning signal indicates that you must check the pressure immediately. Sometimes, a buzzer will notify you of the low air pressure in the tank.

If you are driving a large bus, the low pressure warning signal may go off when the pressure is between 80 and 85 psi.

The compressed air brake system is classified into two systems:

1. **Control System**

The control system controls all the activities in the brake system. It is divided into several parts that include the parking brake circuit, two service brake circuits and the trailer brake circuit.

Going further, the brake circuits are also divided into rear wheel circuits and front wheel circuits. These circuits receive compressed air from the different reservoirs to serve as a source of added safety for the vehicle, especially if there is an air leak.

To apply the service brakes, a brake pedal air valve is used. This valve regulates the rear and front wheel circuits.

The trailer brake is made up of the supply line, marked red, and the blue service line. Through the park brake relay valve, the prime mover park brake air tank provides the supply line with the needed air. The trailer brake relay valve also regulates the control line.

The relay receives operating signals from the trailer service brake hand control, the prime mover brake pedal air valve and the prime mover park brake hand control.

2. **Supply System**

The engine drives the air compressor via a belt or crankshaft pulley. Vehicles use fuel to generate power. That power is distributed to different components of the vehicle through the mechanical and electrical systems. A crankshaft pulley is a major component for power distribution.

Sometimes, the engine may drive the air compressor using timing gears. The engine cooling systems and lubrication ensure that the air compressor is well lubricated. They also help to regulate its temperature.

The compressed air first goes through a cooling coil and then moves to the air dryer. The dryer ensures that the air is moisture-free and removes oil impurities. From the dryer, the compressed air is passed to the supply reservoir where it is stored for use.

The reservoir is otherwise known as the wet tank. From the wet tank, the air is distributed into the secondary reservoir or trailer/front brake reservoir, an auxiliary air supply distribution, the primary or rear brake reservoir and a parking brake reservoir.

Other components of the supply system are pressure limiting, different checks, safety valves and a drain valve.

Dual Air Brake

For increased safety, most commercial vehicles come with dual air brake systems. This system is further separated into two air brake systems. Each of the systems has its own hoses, tanks, lines and other components.

One of the systems controls the brakes at the rear axles while the second system takes care of the front axle, and sometimes, rear axle. The former is referred to as the primary system while the latter is the secondary system. Both of these systems serve as air suppliers to the trailer.

Before you drive a vehicle that comes equipped with a dual air system, it is advisable to allow sufficient time for the air pressure in the air compressor to build up significantly to 100 psi and above in both the secondary and primary systems.

Pay attention to the air pressure gauges or needles in both systems. Don't forget the low air pressure buzzer and warning light.

When the air pressure in both the primary and secondary systems increases to the value recommended by the manufacturer, the buzzer and warning light should go off. That only occurs when the air pressure is above 60 psi.

Both the buzzer and warning light should be triggered before the air pressure goes below 60 psi in either the primary or secondary system. If you experience this while driving, stop driving and park the vehicle in a safe place.

What are the Advantages of Air Brakes over Hydraulic Brakes?

1. It has been previously established that while air brakes are used for heavy commercial vehicles, hydraulic brakes are for lighter automobiles. Air brakes are guaranteed a regular supply of air. Thus, the brake system will always function unlike hydraulic brakes that can run out of fluid, stop working and/or be affected by leaks.
2. In addition to functioning as a medium for force transmission, air brakes also store potential energy while undergoing the compression process.
3. Air brakes have a mechanism that allows them to store enough energy for use in case the compressor fails suddenly.
4. It is easier to attach and detach air line couplings in air brakes than in hydraulic lines. More so, it completely eliminates the possibility of the hydraulic fluid being contaminated by air.
5. You can easily attach and remove air brake circuits on large vehicles such as trailers. This makes it easier to repair faulty circuits.

Disadvantages of Air Brakes

Although air brakes have some attractive features, they also have some weaknesses. These include:

1. They are generally more expensive than hydraulic brakes.
2. They involve higher repair and maintenance costs.
3. Using air brakes involves a more difficult learning curve.
4. Some additional licensing and training (i.e., an endorsement) are needed to drive commercial motor vehicles that use air brakes in the United States.

Air Brakes Inspection

As a commercial motor vehicle driver, it is mandatory that you inspect your air brakes from time to time to identify malfunctioning parts and fix them without delay.

Your checklist should include:

- **Air Compressor Drive Belt:** Check this belt if your vehicle's compressor is driven with a belt. Check its overall condition and tightness.
- **The Slack Adjusters**: You can find the slack adjusters on the vehicle's S-cam brakes. For a thorough inspection of the adjusters, park the vehicle on level ground and ensure that the vehicle remains stationary while you check it.

  To make the slack adjuster movable, release the parking brakes. Pull each slack adjuster very hard with hand gloves. A slack adjuster may need some adjustments if it moves beyond an inch from the point of attachment to the push rod. If you can, adjust it. Otherwise, let a professional handle the adjustment.

  You may find it extremely hard to stop the vehicle if the brake has too much slack. The most common problem associated with brakes is misalignment. This underscores the importance of ensuring that your brakes are properly adjusted.

  If you are driving a post-1994 vehicle, it comes with automatic slack adjustors that become operational when the brakes are fully applied. Nevertheless, checking the slack adjusters regularly can help you to easily identify issues with the adjusters and correct them before it is too late.
- **Brake Discs or Drums, Hoses and Linings:** Brake discs or drums can have cracks. That's expected. However, if the cracks are longer than half the width of the areas allowed for friction, that should be a cause for concern. The longer crack may interfere with the operations of the drums or discs, thereby undermining the efficiency of the brake system. Pay attention to the linings or friction materials too. They mustn't be soaked with grease or oil or be too thin or loose.

  The air hoses that are connected to the brake should be checked too. Rubbing may cause wearing or cutting out and is a problem that must be fixed without delay.
- **The Air Leakage Rate**: You can carry out this test when the air system is fully charged, about 125 psi. Release the parking brake after turning off the engine. Time the rate at which the air pressure drops. If the loss rate is more than 2psi/minute for single vehicles, that's a problem. The figure shouldn't be less than 3 psi/minute for combination vehicles.

  With the brake pedal, apply a minimum of 90 psi. The air pressure mustn't drop more than 3 psi per minute for single vehicles after the initial drop. For combination vehicles, it must not be more than 4 psi.

Check the vehicle for sources of air drop, such as air leaks. If you find any, fix them before operating the vehicle. Otherwise, the brake may malfunction while driving.

- **Test the Service Brakes:** Wait until there is normal air pressure in the service brakes before releasing the parking brake. Then, move the vehicle at about five miles per hour. With the brake pedal, apply the brakes firmly. This test may reveal potential problems that you may otherwise not identify until you need the brakes while driving.
- **Test Low Pressure Warning Signal**: Turn off the engine before you start this test. Make sure that the air pressure is enough that the low pressure warning signal is not already activated. Then, turn the electrical power on. Apply and remove pressure from the brake pedal by stepping on and off it. This will reduce the pressure in the air tank.
  - When the pressure drops below 60 psi in the air tank or less than 60 psi in the air that has the lowest air pressure if the vehicle uses the dual air systems, the warning signal will be activated.
  - This test is necessary to assess the working condition of the low pressure warning signal. A non-functioning low pressure warning signal is dangerous. You may run out of pressure if there is nothing to warn you of that situation. The problem may trigger sudden emergency braking, especially if your vehicle is running on a single-circuit air system.
  - In systems that use a double-circuit air system, it will take a longer time for the vehicle to stop completely. This poses a security risk while driving.
- **Test Parking Brake:** To test this brake, simply stop the vehicle and apply the parking brake. Pull against it gently while the vehicle is in a low gear.

Preventive Maintenance of Air Brake

Air brakes need proper maintenance. Otherwise, they may fail without prior notice. To keep your vehicle's air brakes in the best condition, take these preventive measures:

- If you are driving a bus, make sure the truck is running on 85 pounds psi for its brake system. At that pressure, the brake system will function at optimal capacity and reduce the chances of brake failure and other related issues.
- Check the cut-out governor pressure. The cut-out pressure is about 20 to 25 psi more than the cut-in pressure. For the air compressor, it should read between 120 and 135 psi.
- Consider the air pressure buildup rate. It shouldn't take longer than two minutes for the brake's pressure to rise significantly from 85 psi to 100 psi when working at between 600 and 900 rpm.

- Check the air brake system for water. The condensed air may leave some water as a byproduct. Water can damage the air brake system, especially in areas that are extremely cold. Ice can prevent the brake mechanism from receiving the right amount of air. The wheel can lock up as a result of air being cut off from the brake mechanism. You can prevent this problem by installing automatic drain valves in the air tanks.
- The air brake system is an integral part of a vehicle. Irrespective of the vehicle you operate, you should familiarize yourself with its operations, types and maintenance. A faulty brake system is exceedingly dangerous and could result in your death or in the death of others.

Chapter Two: Hazardous Materials (Hazmat)

Hazmat refers to substances or chemicals that may pose a risk to life, safety and health during transportation. These substances are usually transported in heavy commercial vehicles and a driver must pass a strict test on the safest ways to handle such materials.

Note that some materials are considered hazardous according to the person shipping them and may not actually be hazmat. Conversely, you may consider something non-hazardous when it actually is. Thus, it is imperative that you pay attention to the warning labels on a substance or chemical when transporting it.

It is mandatory for all commercial motor vehicle drivers who transport hazardous materials to take the Hazmat Knowledge test in English. The hazmat endorsement is denoted by an X or H on a CDL. Such drivers must also take a security threat assessment each time they want to renew their CDL.

How to Identify Hazardous Materials

If you transport hazardous materials regularly, make sure you always consider the following:

- Carefully read the shipping paper. If it contains an entry with RQ or X in the appropriate column, you are handling a harmful material. A highlighted entry also denotes dangerous chemicals or materials.
- Be aware of the shipper's line of business whether it's chemical supplies, paint, pest control, fireworks, explosives or agricultural materials. All of these denote potentially hazardous cargo.
- Check the tanks used for transporting the material. Is there hazmat signage or do you see diamond labels indicative of hazmat?
- Are there precautions printed on the materials you want to transport?
- Has the shipper included specific cautions in the shipping documentation?

These are some effective ways you can identify hazardous materials. Once you identify them, take the necessary precautions to transport them.

Hazmat Commercial Driver's License Qualification Requirements

To qualify as a driver who can transport such harmful substances, you are required to satisfy both federal and state government criteria.

These are:

1. Taking a security threat assessment test.
2. Be 18 or above and apply for a CDL.

3. Have a special endorsement that allows you to transport such material. You can't apply for the endorsement if you are below 21.
4. Whenever you renew your CDL, provide the history of licenses you have been issued according to federal law. This is irrespective of the state of residence or the type of license you currently have or have had in the past. The history should go back as far as 10 years.
5. Pass the Transportation Security Administration (TSA) Security Threat Assessment.

The TSA established the 49 CFR 1572 rule on May 5, 2003, to ensure that hazardous substances are properly transported across the country and road users aren't unnecessarily exposed to the harmful effect of such dangerous substances.

The assessment process is relatively simple. A state-approved vendor will fingerprint you. Next, you apply for the TSA assessment either over the phone or online. The TSA will then forward your fingerprints to the FBI. The agency will determine whether or not you have a criminal record. It will send its findings to the TSA who will notify you of the result within two weeks. You are expected to complete the threat assessment within 30 days of submitting your fingerprints.

Any incomplete paperwork or eligibility issues may delay the completion date to enable both you and the TSA to fix potential issues before you are allowed to take the test.

If you have a criminal record and have been convicted in the past, the TSA may permanently disqualify you from getting the hazardous materials endorsement. Some crimes that incur automatic disqualification include sedition, espionage, treason or any other crime that the state or federal government classifies as terrorist-related.

Others that are restricted from taking the test and receiving the endorsement are fugitives, non-US citizens, individuals who are not permanent residents, those who have been medically certified as not mentally competent to handle commercial vehicles or who have involuntarily received medical attention at a mental institution.

The unlawful purchase and transportation of harmful substances, improper transportation of such substances that result in loss of life, disruption of the transportation system, environmental damage or economic disruption are other crimes that disqualify individuals from receiving a hazmat endorsement on their CDL.

You will also be automatically disqualified if you have been convicted of the following crimes in the past:

- Bribery.
- Arson.

- Assault with intent to murder.
- Smuggling.
- Murder.
- Rape or any other form of aggravated sexual abuse.
- Hostage taking.
- Kidnapping.
- Extortion.
- Identity fraud.
- Tax evasion.
- Embezzlement.
- Perjury.

You will also be disqualified if you have not been convicted of any of the crimes listed above but have been acquitted on the grounds of insanity.

Note that you are not allowed to apply for a waiver, nor can you appeal the decision.

You can only appeal a ban on the following grounds:

- A reversed conviction.
- Mistaken identity.

You can apply for a waiver under the following conditions:

- Acknowledgment of conviction based on reason of insanity.
- Acknowledgment of being involuntarily committed to a mental institution.

If you apply for a waiver, the TSA is under obligation to respond to your application within 30 days. However, if there are valid reasons, the TSA can extend the response time at its discretion.

If your appeal or waiver is not granted within the approved time frame, you will be notified of your status. Your state of residence will be notified of your disqualification. If your appeal or waiver is granted, both you and the state will be notified that you are now legally permitted to apply for the endorsement you need for the CDL.

Minor violations such as placarding violations or roadside infractions won't affect your application for a hazmat endorsement nor will they impact your attempts to renew the endorsement.

Hazmat Endorsement Requirements

Hazmat endorsement requirements are as follows:

1. A CDL permit or valid CDL License. When filling out the application form for the endorsement, your permit number should be the same as the one that will be on the CDL.
2. Current proof of identity. If you are a US citizen, the following documents are valid: US passport, certificate of birth issued by a government-approved body, certificate of naturalization or certificate of US citizenship. Either of the two is accepted for naturalized US citizens.
3. A valid Medical Examiner's Certificate (DOT Card). This card is issued to drivers who pass the physical exam. The medical certification process is overseen by the Federal Motor Carrier Safety Administration.

There are three types of hazmat endorsements:

1. **H Endorsement:** This endorsement is for drivers who transport placarded hazardous materials.
2. **N Endorsement:** This endorsement is required to drive a tanker that can transport a minimum of 119 gallons of liquid gas or other hazardous liquids.
3. **X Endorsement:** This is the ultimate endorsement class. With it, you can handle both tanks and other hazardous materials. To receive the endorsement you must pass a test for hazardous materials as well as a skills and knowledge test about tankers.

Cost of Hazmat Endorsement

The TSA charges $86.50 for screening. Your state of residence will then charge additional fees that increase the total cost to $100. Payment is non-refundable and the endorsement is valid for five years. You can make payment with a money order, credit card or certified or company check.

If you are a new applicant and already have a valid Transportation Worker Identification Credential (TWIC) card, you qualify for a reduced rate of $67. The TWIC card is a biometric card that signifies that the applicant has the necessary security clearance to access outer continental shelf facilities, port facilities and some vessels that are regulated by the Maritime Transportation Security Act of 2002.

The act was enacted by the United States Congress in 2002. Its primary objective was to address waterway and port security across the country. It equips the ports with security information that allows them to identify and deter threats.

How to Apply for the TSA

To take the TSA assessment, visit their website and fill out the application form. Some of the information you are required to provide includes:

- Last name.
- First name.
- Middle name.
- Preferred language.
- Gender.
- Date of birth.
- Valid email address.
- Preferred method of contact.
- Country code.
- Phone number.

Note that both the email address and phone number are very important and should be functional and valid. The TSA needs these pieces of information to check your status as well as to confirm your application information when you present yourself for the exam. In the name fields, spaces, letters, apostrophes and hyphens are allowed.

At the TSA's website, use the Enrollment Center Locator to specify where you wish to take the test.

With this simple process, you can choose a location in no time:

- Select a service you wish to enroll.
- Enter your city, zip code and airport code.
- Click "Search" after providing the relevant information.

The CDL Hazmat test is comprised of 30 questions. Candidates are required to get 24 of the answers right (80%) to pass the test.

You may retake the examination as many times as necessary to pass it, paying the examination fee at each retest.

The assessment will test your ability to:

- Identify hazardous materials.
- Placard your vehicle according to established rules.
- Load shipments safely.
- Transport shipments safely.

When you are knowledgeable about correct procedures, you drastically reduce your vulnerability (and the vulnerability of others) to injury from harmful materials and substances. You will also require this knowledge if law enforcement officers stop you and test your knowledge of these materials.

Types of Hazardous Materials

There are nine classes of hazardous materials. These are:

Class 1: Explosives

Explosives include a wide range of materials that can easily detonate when undergoing a chemical reaction. In this class are airbag inflators, ammunition and fireworks.

Class 2: Gases

Gases are substances with vapor pressures of 300 kpa. Compressed cases, aerosols, gas cartridges, fire extinguishers and natural gases fall into this category.

Class 3: Flammable Liquids

Liquids with flashpoints between 60 and 65 degrees Celsius are flammable. They contain mixtures of liquids or have solids in solution. This class includes liquids that are transported at temperatures that are either above or at their flashpoints. Some typical examples of flammable liquids are diesel fuel, some varieties of adhesives, gasoline, alcohol, kerosene and acetone.

Class 5: Organic Peroxides and Oxidizing Substances

This class of hazardous materials includes substances that combust in response to a chemical reaction. Nitrites, chemical oxygen generators and ammonium nitrate fertilizers fall into this category.

Class 6: Infectious and Toxic Substances

Toxic substances can cause harm, injury or death if inhaled or swallowed. They are also harmful if they come into contact with the skin. Substances that contain pathogens are infectious. Included in this class are biological waste, bacteria, tear gas, nicotine, cyanide, biological cultures, arsenic, acids and chloroform.

Class 7: Radioactive Materials

Radioactive materials emit ionizing radiation that is harmful to humans. Radioactive ores and isotopes are some types of radioactive materials that are commonly transported.

Class 8: Corrosives

Corrosives disintegrate other materials through a chemical reaction. If they leak during transportation, they will damage whatever material they come in contact with. Acid solutions, dyes, acids, paints, batteries and flux are all considered corrosive.

Class 9: Miscellaneous Hazardous Materials

Hazardous materials in this category are those that don't fall into any of the other eight classes. Genetically modified organisms, substances that are transported at high temperatures, environmentally hazardous substances and magnetized materials are in the miscellaneous class. Class 9 materials include life-saving appliances, dry ice, first aid kits, lithium-ion batteries, fuel cell engines and vehicles.

While transporting hazardous materials, take extra precautions that will guarantee your life and that of others. Your vehicle should be in great condition and you should abide by all rules and regulations guiding your operations.

Understanding the basic requirements for operating a hazmat vehicle will enhance your chances of being licensed to operate one.

Chapter Three: Combination Vehicles

There is an increasing demand for drivers who can handle a wide range of heavy vehicles. If you can handle several types of trucks, you have increased chances of getting a job as a truck driver. However, you must pass the Combination Vehicle test as a prerequisite for obtaining the license.

Combination vehicles have some unique properties that distinguish them from other types of vehicles. They are longer, heavier, and due to their weight and size, require better driving skills and experience than single commercial vehicles.

Thus, if you are preparing to drive combination vehicles, your driving experience and knowledge must be top notch. You must understand the basic driving skills and safety precautions that apply to these specific types of vehicles. Hence, it is imperative that you take the CDL Combination Vehicle test.

Requirements for Combination Vehicles Endorsement

If you want to add the Combination Vehicles endorsement to your CDL, you must understand that each state has its own unique testing process.

Before you take the driving test, you must take the written test first. This chapter discusses what the test entails and provides practical tips to help you successfully pass the exam.

A combination vehicle is otherwise known as a semitruck or semi. It's a combination of a tractor unit and a trailer or more. The connection between the tractor and the trailer(s) is done with a converter dolly or fifth-wheel dolly. Sometimes, two dollies can be used.

The fifth wheel plays a major role in the combination vehicle. Without this connector, a combination vehicle can't bend in the middle, creating a problem for drivers.

Safety Concerns

A combination vehicle driver must take some safety precautions when handling the vehicle. This is due to the increased complication of operating such vehicles in comparison with a straight truck. Ensure you are familiar with the following safety measures:

1. **Braking**

It usually takes longer to stop an empty truck than a fully loaded one because you are more vulnerable to jackknifing.

Jackknifing occurs when a vehicle becomes out of sync with its attached trailer and thus bends into a V or an L shape, skidding uncontrollably. Loss of traction is usually the major factor behind this problem.

Loss of traction occurs when there is low friction between the tire and the road. This may be caused by gravel, sand, ice, snow or any other substance that causes tires to lose their grip on the road surface. You may also experience loss of traction if you turn the wheels too sharply.

To prevent jackknifing:

- Be extra careful when driving on light roads. Since this problem is common to empty trailers or trailers with badly distributed loads that limit traction, don't apply strong brakes when driving empty trailers.
- When driving on a curve, avoid braking suddenly or decelerating sharply. If you must apply the brakes or decelerate, do that before you get to the curve.
- Rather than apply the brakes suddenly, brake progressively while you simultaneously reduce your speed gradually to avoid jackknifing.
- Avoid skidding as much as you can. Skidding is usually the first step towards jackknifing. If your vehicle does start skidding, release the brake while correcting the skid simultaneously.
- Always check your trailer in the mirrors. If you can see your trailer through your mirror, that is an indication that it is skidding. If this occurs, let go of the brakes immediately. Do whatever you can to bring the vehicle under control.

You can avoid all forms of braking-related problems by being aware of your environment when driving. This allows you to avoid situations that may trigger braking problems.

Avoid panic stops as much as possible. They increase the chances of braking problems because it takes longer to stop large vehicles than smaller ones.

2. **Turn Wide**

You are less likely to have safety issues with your vehicle when traveling in a straight line than when negotiating a bend. In a straight-line motion, the steering wheels determine the path the wheels will take.

When a vehicle is negotiating a bend, the rear wheels don't follow the steering wheels but take a different path, or a "shortcut." This is known in the trucking industry as off-tracking or cheating. The off-tracking is more pronounced in longer trucks than shorter ones.

If you don't control your vehicle properly, off-tracking may cause a major problem. A preventive measure against this problem is to focus on the front wheels and steer them wide enough to make allowance for the rear wheels to move freely without skidding.

Note, however, that the swinging shouldn't be so wide that it creates a gap between the curb and the trailer. Too wide of a gap may force other drivers to take the unnecessary risk of getting in between the curb and the trailer's rear. Some drivers may want to pass your vehicle on the right as well, thereby constituting a big risk to the swinging.

If it doesn't seem possible to make a complete turn from your lane, turn wide while completing the turn and not before you start it. That move will allow you to complete the turn as safely as possible.

3. Railroad Tracks

Railroad tracks are another safety concern for drivers of combination vehicles. If you are pulling a trailer with low clearance, you should be especially careful about railroad tracks.

Some pieces of equipment such as lowboy trailers and car carriers are more prone to getting stuck when traveling over railroad tracks.

You can avoid this problem as follows:

- While crossing railroad tracks, don't shift gears.
- Avoid stopping your vehicle on railroad tracks.

If you do find your vehicle stuck on railroad tracks, get out immediately. Look for a DOT placard that includes an emergency number (800). Call this number immediately for assistance and stay away from the vehicle.

4. Backing Up

Backing up a combination vehicle is one of several critical skills you need to become a combination vehicle driver. The National Safety Council reports that approximately 25% of vehicle accidents can be attributed to poor backing up. Over 500 deaths and 15,000 injuries are caused by reverse-related accidents.

The US National Highway Traffic Safety Administration reports that most accidents that occur during backing up occur in parking lots and residential driveways. More so, the driver is always considered at fault when such an accident occurs.

The following tips will help you to master the skill and get your Combination Vehicle Endorsement:

- Use the G.O.A.L approach. Don't rush while backing up. Rather, take it slowly. Always Get Out And Look at your surroundings to enable you to avoid obstacles.
- Don't back up unless it is absolutely necessary. You should do anything possible to avoid backing up. This may include parking in spaces that allow you to get out without the need to reverse first.
- Walk around the vehicle when necessary. This will give you a firsthand view of your environment, especially potential limitations that may make reversing more difficult. During the walk, pay attention to potholes, muddy areas and other potential dangers you should avoid. Check for low-hanging trees, obstructions and other related problems.
- If you can get someone to assist you, do so. With the assistance of a spotter, you won't have issues with reversing the vehicle.
  When using a spotter, both of you should communicate with hand signals rather than verbal signals.
- Before you start backing up, honk your horn twice. This is to notify other road users or passersby and avoid preventable accidents. The horn will draw people's attention to your vehicle as well as enable them to know the direction you are coming from.
- When backing up, consider the distance. The longer the distance, the more vulnerable you are.
- Choose a parking space with an easy exit. Avoid spaces where you may be crowded by other vehicles. As much as possible, park in the center of a parking spot.
- When backing up, look at your mirror at intervals of three to five seconds.
- Pay attention to your speed. Back up as slowly as you can.
- Check all the clearances. These are the front, right side, rear, ground, left side and overhead.
- Pay attention to how you steer. Remember that the trailer is steered by the tractor. When you steer the vehicle to the right, the trailer's rear will go to the left and vice versa.
- Keep your window down so that you can hear your spotter, if you use one, and other warnings. If you roll your windows up, you may not hear such warnings.

The tips above offer some temporary solutions to backing up issues. Some long-term solutions include:

- Practice regularly. You can't get backing up right if you don't practice regularly.
- Install rear-vision cameras in your vehicles. Your problems with rear blind spots are solved once you have full visual control of your vehicle's rear while backing up.

5. **Rollover Risks**

It is estimated that truck rollovers are responsible for over half of truck rollover-related driver deaths.

A rollover is usually the result of a common loading error in trucks. When a truck carries more cargo than it is intended to carry, it has a higher center of gravity. This destabilizes the truck and makes it easier to turn over.

You can combat rollover risk by doing the following:

- Keep the cargo very close to the ground. This is a very important driving tip for combination vehicle drivers. When the center of gravity is close to the ground, rolling over is minimized.
  Also, remember to keep the cargo more in the center than on the sides. This prevents the vehicle from learning towards the side where the load is more concentrated.
- When approaching turns, drive slowly. Rollovers are common to drivers who drive too fast and turn abruptly when driving around corners. If you are driving off ramps or on ramps, drive slowly too.
- When you are fully loaded and need to change lanes, do so slowly. Changing lanes quickly may destabilize your vehicle.

6. **Rearward Amplification**

A common problem with trucks with trailers is known as the "crack-the-whip" effect. This usually occurs when a trailer changes lanes quickly. This can result in a turnover. A turnover can be very dangerous, especially when it affects other vehicles.

This usually occurs when a truck-trailer or any other longer combination vehicle has to make sharp maneuvers when traveling at a high speed, usually at above 80 km/hr. Sometimes, this need is caused when the driver is trying to avoid colliding with other objects and decides to change lanes swiftly. During a swift lane change, the last trailer is usually the most susceptible to turnover.

7. **Braking Performance**

Braking-related problems are another huge safety concern you must deal with as a combination vehicle driver. Several factors determine the braking performance of a vehicle. This includes friction between the road and tires, the vehicle's aerodynamic resistance and a host of other factors.

Longer combination vehicles don't have a similar braking wire system as shorter vehicles. The complexity of the wire system can affect the braking performance negatively. This makes longer vehicles more prone to braking problems than other vehicles.

Antilock Brake Systems

The antilock braking system is a special safety system in automobiles that prevents their wheels from becoming locked up during braking. This enables the driver to be in control of the steering and makes stopping easier.

Also known as the antiskid braking system, it allows the wheels to maintain contact with the ground, preventing uncontrollable skid such as on a slippery road.

In the United States, all converter dollies and trailers built from March 1, 1998, must have the Antilock Brake System. This braking system is designed to solve some of the braking-related problems that are common to most long vehicles.

How does ABS Work?

Antilock Brakes work on a simple theory. When a wheel skids, its traction is reduced considerably in comparison with a non-skidding wheel. A typical scenario is when you get stuck while driving on ice. The reduced traction causes spinning, making braking more difficult.

The ABS prevents this braking problem. It keeps the wheels from skidding when you try to slow the vehicle down. This is beneficial because it helps you to stop the vehicle faster without losing control.

When the computer controlling the ABS senses impending wheel lockup, it reduces the braking pressure until it is safe enough to enable you to control the vehicle with ease. It supports the normal braking system by activating the wheels when an impending lockup is sensed.

Regardless of the existence of the ABS on either a trailer, a tractor or both, use the same braking process. Monitor the trailer and tractor while slowing down. Don't forget to release the brakes when necessary to help you to stay in control.

Sometimes, the ABS may malfunction. If that happens, don't panic because you can still stop the vehicle with the regular brakes. Use them while driving cautiously.

The ABS has four major components:

1. **Valves:** Each of the brakes controlled by the antilock system has a brake line. In the brake line is a valve responsible for regulating the air pressure supplied to the brakes when ABS is in action.

The valve can be in three different positions:

- In the first position, it is open and allows the transfer of pressure to the brakes from the master cylinder.
- The valve is closed in the second position. There is a constraint of pressure to the brakes from the master cylinder as the brake valve is closed.
- In the third position, the valve releases a fraction of pressure on the brakes until the vehicle is completely stopped.

When you suddenly brake at high speeds, you will feel a resistance. This is the brake valves at work. They are controlling the pressure that the master cylinder transferred to the brakes.

2. **Speed Sensor:** The speed sensor determines the acceleration and deceleration needed by the wheels by monitoring their speed.
   The speed sensor consists of a wire coil or magnet assembly and an exciter which is a V-shaped teeth ring. The assembly generates the electricity needed for the monitoring when the exciter passes in front of the assembly.
3. **Electronic Control Unit (ECU):** This is an electronic control unit whose job description includes receiving, amplifying and filtering the sensor signals. Its operations on the sensor signals allow it to calculate the wheel acceleration and rotational speed. The sensors in the circuit send a signal to the ECU that it uses to control the brake pressure.
4. **Hydraulic Control Unit (HCU):** The ECU sends a signal to the Hydraulic Control Unit ordering it to either release or apply the brakes according to the antilock conditions. The HCU then increases the hydraulic pressure to control the brakes. It can also do this by reducing the braking power and bypassing the pedal force.
5. **Controller:** The controller controls the ABS valves and watches the speed sensors as well.
6. **Pump:** This component is designed to return some of the pressure the valve releases from the brakes. This ensures that there is always enough pressure in the brakes.
   The controller consistently monitors the speed sensors. It looks for some special declaration in the vehicle's wheel. When it notices this, it locks the wheels. With locked wheels, the vehicle will stop spinning faster than when the wheels are allowed to stop spinning on their own.

Thus, ABS modifies the fluid pressure in the brake, regardless of the amount of pressure you apply, with the objective of putting the speed of the wheel on a level that makes optimal braking performance achievable.

When driving on a slippery surface, it is easier for an average driver to stop quickly with the assistance of ABS than for a professional driver to stop without it.

There are five types of combination vehicles:

1. **Rocky Mountain Doubles:** This is a combination of two trailers of different sizes. The first is a 40-foot trailer combined with a 28-foot trailer or pup. A pup trailer is between 26 and 29 feet long. Such trailers are used extensively in doubles and triples.
2. **Turnpike Double:** This double is a combination of two trailers with equal sizes, usually each 40 feet or as long as 53 feet each.
3. **STAA Doubles Pup**: In this category are two 28.5-foot trailers.
4. **Triple Trailer:** As the name suggests, this combination vehicle type is made up of three trailers. Each trailer is 28.5 feet long.
5. **B-Train:** B-trains have twin trailers that are each up to 33 feet. The trailers use the same wheel set between the back trailer and the front trailer.

Types of ABS

The Antilock Braking System is classified based on two factors: brakes and sensors. The number of channels is another important factor that defines the number of valves that are controlled and how many speed sensors the system has. The major types of ABS are:

1. **Four-channel and four-sensor ABS**

As the name implies, this type of ABS contains four channels and the same number of sensors. Each of the four wheels has a speed sensor and valve too. The setup makes it possible for the controller to monitor each wheel with ease. The focused monitoring ensures that the braking system can work at maximum capacity.

2. **Three-channel and three-sensor ABS**

Each of the three front wheels in this setup has a valve and a speed sensor. Each of the rear wheels also has a sensor and a valve. You can locate the rear wheels' speed sensors in the rear axle.

Most modern heavy vehicles are equipped with ABS and it is considered a must-have safety feature. According to recent research, these vehicles are less likely to be involved in accidents than other cars without the braking system because drivers can still control their vehicles with ease.

Benefits of ABS

The Antilock Braking System offers drivers the following benefits:

- It offers stability while maneuvering the vehicle.
- It makes the steering controllable during emergency braking.

- Braking distance is considerably reduced.
- It prevents emergency-braking-triggered tire damage.
- It helps drivers to avoid wheel lockup.

Always remember these safety tips if your vehicle comes equipped with ABS:

- ABS won't shorten a stopping distance although it will assist you with controlling a vehicle.
- The braking system shouldn't change your normal braking method. Your vehicle will ideally stop when brakes are applied normally. ABS will only assist you to control the vehicle when the wheels are locked up due to over-braking.
- ABS is not a replacement for your regular brakes.
- If you have poor brake maintenance or drive with bad brakes, ABS won't compensate for such shortcomings.
- ABS won't prevent your vehicle from turning skids, although it can prevent brake-induced skids.

Coupling and Uncoupling

Your coupling and uncoupling skills will be tested. Knowing how to uncouple and uncouple a combination vehicle correctly is one of the most basic skills you need in order to ensure its safe operation.

You run a great risk if you either couple or uncouple a vehicle incorrectly. If a part disengages or falls off while the vehicle is in motion, that can lead to a serious accident.

For correct coupling and uncoupling:

- Check the vehicle for missing or damaged parts. If there are any, replace them immediately.
- Check the mounting to the tractor. Is it secure? If it isn't, that poses a security risk that you should avoid at all costs.
- Ensure that you grade the fifth-wheel plate as required. Steering problems may arise from unnecessary friction between the trailer and the tractor if the fifth-wheel plate is not well lubricated.
- Check the position of the fifth-wheel vehicle as well. This includes checking whether the safety unlocking handle is in a position that guarantees automatic locking. The trailer kingpin shouldn't be broken or bent. The jaws should be open.
- Inspect the area around the vehicle. Is the area clear of any obstruction? What about the trailer wheels? Make sure that the spring brakes are on while the

wheels are chocked. If the vehicle carries cargo, secure it properly. To avoid rollover, make sure it won't bulge or move when coupling the trailer.
- How you position the vehicle is also important. When handling a tractor, put it in front of the trailer directly. Don't forget that you should only back under the trailer directly for security reasons. Backing under it at an angle may lead to accidentally pushing the trailer, an action that can roll the trailer over or break the landing gear.
- Each combination vehicle comes with a coupling and uncoupling manual. Refer to it for further information.

The steps discussed above are for general coupling and this may differ from one combination vehicle to another.

Inspecting Combination Vehicles

Most of the problems associated with combination vehicles are preventable to a reasonable degree. However, you must identify such problems and fix them before they rear their ugly heads.

This underscores the importance of a proper inspection. When you inspect the vehicle, you may stumble upon some potential problems and can then fix them without delay. A thorough inspection of your vehicle should be done with a focus on the following areas:

1. **Check the Coupling System Area**

When checking the coupling system areas, pay attention to the following parts:
The fifth wheel:

- Check the lower section and see if the fifth wheel is properly secured to the frame. Are there missing or damaged parts?
- Check whether there is a visible space between the lower and upper sections of the wheel.
- Check the locking jacks. These should be around the shank and not at the head of the kingpin.
- Finally, take a look at the release arm. Is it properly locked or not? What about the safety lock/latch? Is it fully engaged?

Check the upper section of the fifth wheel: Your focus here is on the kingpin and glide plate.

- How is the glide plate mounted to the trailer frame? Is it securely mounted or not?
- Check the kingpin's condition.

The sliding fifth wheel:

- Check for any damaged or missing parts.
- Check if the slide is properly greased.

  Some of them are air-powered. If so, check for air leaks too. Also, take a look at the locking pins. Are they properly locked in place?

Check the air and electric lines: The trailer has some electric and air lines; check these as well.

- Start from the electrical cord and ensure that it is firmly plugged in the right places and well secured.
- Also, check the air lines for damage such as air leaks.
- Ensure that the air lines and gland hands are properly connected. There shouldn't be room for air leaks. Leave enough rooms for turns by using the right amount of slack.

2. **The Landing Gear**

A general inspection of a combination vehicle should cover the landing gear too.

- Check the landing gear for missing parts and to see if it is damaged, bent and fully raised or not.
- Check the crank handle's position and security.

When handling power-operated landing gear, your focus should be on the hydraulics.

- Check to see if there are hydraulic or air leaks. If so, fix them immediately.

It is important that you carry out a comprehensive inspection of your vehicle. Identifying issues and fixing them as soon as possible is a preventive measure against accidents that may be triggered by missing or damaged parts.

3. **Check the Brakes**

A brake check is undoubtedly one of the most important ways you can prevent unfortunate accidents. The brakes should be in perfect condition before you drive the vehicle.

The check should cover the following areas of the brake:

- Airflow to the trailers must be smooth. If the flow is interfered with, the trailer will be deprived of one of the basic things it needs for optimum performance.
- Check the tractor protection valve. First, charge the air brake system. Then, shut off the engine and reduce the air pressure in the air tank by stepping the brake pedal on and off several times. When you do this, the tractor protection valve control, otherwise known as the trailer air supply control, will change position from “normal” to “emergency” when the air pressure falls into the specified pressure range by the manufacturer. This is usually between 20 to 45 psi.

  If the protection valve malfunctions, the tractor may lose its air through a brake leak or an air hose. In either case, the emergency brakes will come on and this may lead to a loss of control of the vehicle.
- Check if the air pressure in the trailer service brakes is normal. Then, let go of the parking brakes and slowly move the vehicle forward.
- Test the emergency brakes. Start the trailer emergency brake test by charging the air trailer air brake system first. Then, once it is fully charged, check the trailer and see if it rolls freely or with difficulty. Stop the air supply control and pull it out. Alternatively, put the air supply control in the emergency position. Check if the emergency brakes are on.

When preparing for the combination vehicle test, learn as much as you can about the vehicle. Be aware of existing regulations and abide by them. Perform routine vehicle maintenance. Your knowledge of this aspect of combination vehicles will also be tested.

Chapter Four: Doubles and Triples

Doubles and triples, also known as Longer Combination Vehicles (LCVs), refer to a combination vehicle system where a truck has multiple trailers attached to it. This is quite different from the standard commercial vehicle system.

You need a separate endorsement to pull multiple trailers simultaneously. Thus, to be licensed to drive doubles and triples you are required to pass a specific assessment that tests your practical and theoretical knowledge of LCVs.

The weight limits and length of these vehicles vary from state to state and some of these LCVs can only be driven on turnpikes or highways.

The trucking industry offers more job opportunities for truck drivers who can handle doubles or triples. Once you get endorsements for these types of vehicles, you can use your skills both on regional and local routes.

Note that some states have stiff restrictions on triples. However, a growing number of these states are relaxing their rules to make more room for triple trailers. Thus, when you get the doubles or triples endorsement, you open yourself to additional job opportunities in the truck industry.

How to Pass the Doubles or Triples Endorsement Test

Each state conducts its own licensing examination for drivers seeking endorsements for double or triple vehicles. However, federal regulation of the industry ensures that the required examination for endorsement covers the same subjects across the country.

The test covers the following topics:

1. **Assembly procedures:** You are required to understand the assembly procedure for the type of vehicle you are driving. Thus, when you uncouple the vehicle for any reason, you must be able to re-couple it as well.
2. **Potential problems:** What are the potential problems that may arise when operating a double or triple? You must have comprehensive knowledge of these problems and how to solve them. Sometimes, though, you may need the assistance of a professional to fix issues that are beyond your knowledge.
3. **Handling:** During the test, your ability to operate the vehicle, irrespective of the challenges you may face, will be assessed.

Doubles and Triples Endorsement Requirements

Remember that the requirements for this endorsement vary slightly from state to state. Before you take the test in any state, you must pay either a licensing or testing fee. Some states charge both fees.

Your location determines where you take the test. While some states allow CDL drivers to take the test at a third-party site, others make it mandatory for drivers to take the test at the local DMV. Thus, you must understand the rules in your state before applying to take the exam.

Pulling Double or Triple Trailers

Pulling double or triple trailers can be both challenging and risky due to the sheer weight, size and length of the trailers. Various things can go wrong because these vehicles are renowned for their instability in comparison to other types of vehicles. While driving LCVs, you should always:

1. Take practical steps to prevent the trailer from rolling over. As a safety precaution, drive slowly and steer the vehicle gently when driving off ramps, around corners, curves or on ramps. What is considered a safe speed for a single-trailer combination vehicle or a straight truck on a curve may be too much for doubles or triples. So, drive as slowly as possible.
2. Be aware that the crack-the-whip effect is more pronounced with doubles and triples than other types of combination vehicles. This effect can cause a trailer to overturn when a driver makes a quick lane change. In some cases, only the trailer will turn over while the tractor remains unaffected.

   Therefore, it is imperative that you steer gently when handling such vehicles. Note, also, that the part of a double or triple that is most likely to turn over is the last trailer.
3. Thoroughly inspect the vehicle. Although this is time-consuming in view of the various parts you must check in a double or a triple, taking the time to inspect the vehicle could be life-saving. As previously mentioned, a comprehensive inspection will allow you to identify potential problems before they cause an accident.
4. Pay attention to space. Doubles and triples are longer and bigger than most combination vehicles. Hence, they need more space to operate since you can't stop or turn them as suddenly as smaller vehicles. Thus, when following other vehicles, leave enough space between you and them. When crossing or entering traffic, make sure you have enough space to maneuver your vehicle.
5. Manage adverse conditions well. When driving doubles or triples, you may sometimes have to drive in bad weather and other adverse conditions such as slippery roads. When driving in the mountains you must be especially careful to prevent loss of traction, skidding and rollover.
6. Consider how you park the vehicle. Smaller vehicles can drive in and out of a parking lot with ease. However, you can't handle a heavy double or triple trailer in the same manner. Thus, when parking, take several factors into consideration, such as the

number of vehicles in the parking lot. You don't want to miscalculate a space and get stuck between vehicles.

You can avoid some of the most common problems that are associated with doubles and triples if you take the above tips into consideration when operating them. By identifying potential problems before they rear their ugly heads, it's easy to fix them and protect yourself from unfortunate accidents.

Coupling and Uncoupling Double/Triple Trailers

Your coupling and uncoupling knowledge will also be tested on the test. Knowledge of how to correctly couple and uncouple your vehicle ensures that you don't put yourself and other road users at risk if you drive a badly coupled vehicle.

To couple a double trailer:

- Secure the rear trailer. If there are no spring brakes in the second trailer, drive the tractor very close to the trailer. Then, connect the emergency line. After charging the trailer air tank, carefully disconnect the emergency line to engage the trailer emergency brakes.

  If you have some reservations about the brakes, chock the wheels to prevent the trailer from rolling forward or backward while coupling or uncoupling it.

  When connecting semitrailers, make sure that the one with the heaviest load is connected immediately behind the tractor. The lighter trailer should be connected last to ensure safe handling of the vehicle.
- You can couple a semitrailer to the rear of a tractor with a converter gear on a dolly. Place the converter dolly in front of the rear trailer. Open the air tank petcock to release the dolly brakes. Connect the dolly to the trailer first. Move the dolly connector to the first semitrailer's rear to connect the two. Then, lock the pintle hook and while the dolly is in a raised position, secure it.

  After securing the dolly support, pull in close to the front of the second semitrailer and lower it. Then, unhook the dolly from the first trailer and wheel it in front of the second trailer. Make sure that the dolly and the kingpin are in line with each other.
- Connect the dolly to the trailer in front. Place the first semitrailer in front of the converter dolly and hook it to the front trailer by locking the pintle hook and securing the converter gear support while in a raised position.
- Connect the dolly to the rear trailer. Before you start, chock the wheels or lock the trailer brakes. Then move the dolly under the rear trailer. Raise the dolly slightly

to prevent damage to the landing gear that may be caused if the trailer moves unexpectedly.

Pull the coupling against the second semitrailer's pin to test it. After the test, check the coupling manually and make sure that there are no spaces between the lower and upper fifth wheel. The locking jaws should be closed on the kingpin. You can then connect the air hoses, safety chains and light cords. Once you are done with that, close the air tank petcock. The second trailer's rear valves should be shut off too.

After closing the valves, check the first trailer's rear and open the shutoff valves. Do the same for the dolly if it has such valves too. Then, raise the landing gear as much as possible.

Charge the brakes by pushing in the air supply knob. Check the second trailer for air by opening the emergency line shutoff. If there is no air pressure, the brakes won't work, which will tell you something is wrong.

You also need to know how to uncouple a double or triple combination vehicle.
To uncouple the rear trailer:

- Park the rig on firm and level ground. The rig should be in a straight line.
- To prevent the rig from moving, use the parking brakes.
- If the second trailer doesn't have spring brakes, chock its wheels.
- Remove some weight from the dolly by lowering the second trailer's landing gear. The landing gear is a retractable support that comes in handy to keep a trailer stable when its tractor has been removed. It supports the second trailer and keeps it off the dolly.
- If the dolly has air shutoffs, shut them off. Do the same for those on the first semitrailer's rear.
- Secure all the electric lines and dolly air after disconnecting them. Then, release the dolly brakes and the fifth-wheel latch.
- Pull the first semitrailer forward slowly from the rear semitrailer's rear, followed by the dolly.

To uncouple the converter dolly:

- Lower the dolly's landing gear and disconnect all the safety chains.
- Chock the wheels. Alternatively, you can apply the gear spring brakes.
- Release the first semitrailer's pintle hook and move away from the dolly slowly.

A note of caution: When the dolly is under the rear trailer, don't unlock or detach its pintle hook. In most cases, the trailer's weight makes the right hitch fly up and can cause damage.

You should also note that there are some differences between coupling and uncoupling a double and a triple. It is advisable to check the manufacturer's handbook when you are in doubt about the best way to couple or uncouple either of the two.

Coupling a Triple Trailer

When coupling a triple trailer, follow the same procedure as you would to couple a double. However, some extra steps are needed for a complete coupling:

- Couple the second and third trailers first.
- Uncouple the tractor and pull it away from the trailers.
- Following the standard procedure, couple the first semitrailer and the tractor.
- Once you are done with that, couple the first semitrailer and tractor to the second and third trailers.

Uncoupling Triple Trailers

Uncoupling triple trailers is relatively easy. First, pull out the dolly and unhitch it. Then unhitch the third trailer the same way you would a double trailer.

Doubles and Triples Inspection

Checking your vehicle is a part of your job description to ensure that every part functions properly before you begin driving. As a double or triple driver, you should always check the following parts of your vehicle:

1. **Coupling Areas**
    - Check the lower section of the fifth wheel and see if it's mounted to the frame securely. Also inspect the parts for damage or missing parts.
    - Check the wheel's lubrication.
    - Take a look at the lower and upper fifth wheel. Are there spaces between them? If yes, that's a red flag.
    - Check the locking jaws to ensure they are around the shank and not the kingpin's head.

Finally, inspect the release arm to ensure it is well seated and locked properly.

When you are done with the lower part of the fifth wheel, check the upper part as well.

- The trailer frame should have the glide plate securely mounted on it. Otherwise, there is an issue with the mounting that needs urgent attention.
- Check the kingpin for signs of damage.

- Check the electrical cord to ensure it is plugged in firmly and well secured.
- Check all the lines, both air and electrical, for signs of damage.
- Slide the fifth wheel and check if the slide has any missing or damaged parts. How lubricated is the slide? What about the locking pins? Does it have them? Are they firmly locked in place? If your vehicle uses an air-powered fifth-wheel slide, check for signs of air leaks.
- Also check the distance between the tractor frame and the fifth wheel. They shouldn't be so far apart that they hit each other during turns. The same applies to the cab; it shouldn't hit the trailer while turning.
- Inspect the landing gear for missing or bent parts. How raised is the landing gear? Optimally, the landing gear should be fully raised. If not, check for possible problems. If your vehicle comes with power-operated landing gear, check for hydraulic or air leaks.
- Check the crank handle to ensure it is secured and in the right place.

2. **Air Brake Check**
   A correctly working air brake is lifesaving and prevents injuries.
   As such, to keep your brake in the best condition, check it regularly for errors and worn-out parts.

   a. The trailer emergency brakes should always be in perfect condition. Check to ensure they have the right air pressure. Also, check the emergency brakes by charging the air brake system and seeing if the trailer rolls freely. Then, stop the trailer air supply control and pull it out. The air supply control, as the name implies, supplies air to the trailer. When you push it in, it supplies the air. It shuts off the air when you pull it out.

      You can also place the air supply control in the emergency position to check its performance. The air supply control is otherwise known as the trailer emergency valve or tractor protection valve control.

   b. Regular airflow to the trailer is necessary for effective braking. Ensure that nothing interferes with it. To check the airflow, put the trailer in a stationary position using the tractor parking brake. Alternatively, chock the wheels. Wait until the air pressure reaches normal before pushing in the trailer air supply knob. Air should be immediately supplied to the emergency supply lines. Then, supply the needed air to the service line with the trailer handbrake. If everything goes smoothly, this indicates there are no issues with the airflow. Otherwise, correct any problems detected during the test.

   c. The trailer service brake is needed intermittently to slow down and stop the vehicle. Check to ensure it's in good condition. Pay attention to the parking brakes. Release them and move the vehicle forward to test them. With the hand control or trolley valve, apply the brakes to ensure they function properly. Check the air pressure too. You may need a professional to handle issues with the trailer service brake if you can't fix an error you identify.

d. The tractor protection valve is designed to protect the tractor air brake system whenever there is a serious problem such as a severe air leak or trailer breakaway. Aside from that, you can use the valve to stop airflow to the trailer before you disconnect the lines when the pressure drops between 20 psi and 45 psi.
Thus, issues with the protection valve can affect the overall performance of the air brake system. Hence, always check the air pressure and other parts to ensure that the tractor protection valve is in good shape.

Getting the appropriate endorsement for driving doubles or triples can be pretty easy if you are knowledgeable about LCVs' various aspects. Take some time to understand the practical aspect of the test in addition to the theoretical. Then, you will be in a better position to ace the test.

Chapter Five: Tanker License

Tanker drivers across the United States are required to have the appropriate endorsement for their CDL. The Federal Motor Carrier Safety Administration (FMCSA) established some rules that are designed to ensure the safety of both tanker drivers and other road users.

The FMCSA is an arm of the United States Department of Transportation. It regulates the country's entire trucking industry. Its primary mission is to reduce the number of injuries, crashes and fatalities that are caused by large buses and trucks.

Established on January 1, 2000, the Motor Carrier Safety Improvement Act of 1999 emphasized the importance of road safety measures with a view to making the roadways safer for both drivers and the general public. It made it illegal to drive commercial vehicles that carry a large quantity of gaseous or liquid content without proper training and endorsement.

Tankers include flatbeds, dry vans, box trucks and reefers. If you drive any of these vehicles, you must have a tanker endorsement.

Tanker Eligibility Requirements

You must have a tanker endorsement under any of the following conditions:

- The containers you are transporting are not loaded.
- Your vehicle carries gaseous or liquid containers that can contain more than 119 gallons.
- The total volume of the containers' content exceeds 1,000 gallons.
- The tanker's content is immaterial. Regardless of whether you transport hazardous material with it or not, once it meets any of the requirements above, driving it without a tanker endorsement is a violation of federal law.

There are some exceptions to the rule, though. Under the following conditions, you don't need the tanker endorsement to drive a commercial vehicle, even if it shares the same shape and design with a tanker:

- It is a temporary attachment to a flatbed trailer.
- The tank is not designed for transporting goods.
- The tank is empty.
- The trailer is not a tanker.

Also, note that you can drive an empty tank if you have a CLP with a tank endorsement. Furthermore, if the tanker has previously been used to transport a hazardous material but the tank has been well cleaned and purged, you can drive it with a CLP.

A tanker can only carry a specific amount of liquid. The amount is dependent on several factors such as:

- The maximum weight limit that the government allows on public roads.
- The expansion rate plays a significant role in the quantity of a liquid that can be transported at a given time. During loading, the driver must make allowances to allow the liquid to expand without spilling.
  Since different liquids expand at different rates, you must be familiar with the expansion rate of the specific liquid you are transporting and make necessary provisions for it.
- You can't exceed the volume capacity of a tank. For example, a tank that is designed to transport 1,000 gallons can't exceed that value.
- The Gross Combination Weight Rating (GCWR) of a truck refers to the maximum allowed combined mass of the vehicle which includes both the cargo and the passengers. For a tanker, this is the combined mass of the passengers in the tanker as well as the tank's contents. The Gross Combination Weight Rating is also known as Gross Combination Mass (GCM), Maximum Authorized Mass (MAM) and Gross Train Weight.

Some loads are at the maximum weight limit, even before the tank is filled up. In such cases, the tank can't be fully loaded. The space left in the tank will worsen the surge problem common to tankers.

Since March 2017, it is a criminal offense in any state for any tanker driver to operate a tanker without the right authorization.

The FMCSA has a stiff penalty for drivers caught violating the rule. If you are a commercial tanker driver and operate your vehicle without the necessary endorsement while carrying cargo that warrants the endorsement, you will be penalized $5,000. Your license may also be suspended for about 90 days.

The regulation is necessary in view of the sheer size of a tanker. Tankers are large and heavy. Thus, their drivers need special skills to handle them. Tankers require special inspection, maintenance and safety procedures.

How to Get a Tanker Endorsement

Every tanker driver must visit the local DMV to apply to take the Tanker Endorsement Knowledge Test.
With the application, you will be required to pay a test fee, between $10 and $50, depending on the state.

Safety and Security Concerns for Tanker Drivers

Driving a heavy vehicle such as a tanker comes with its own challenges:

1. **Rollover Risk**

Commercial vehicles, including tankers, are known for their high center of gravity, unlike smaller vehicles. Tankers top the list of commercial vehicles with the highest centers of gravity. Thus, such vehicles are always at a high risk of rolling over.

2. **Bulkheads**

Bulkhead-related issues are one of the most common problems with tankers. A bulkhead is a barrier or a dividing wall between the compartments in the tank. It is used for dividing large tanks into smaller tanks. These tanks are slightly different from each other, volume wise. Hence, each small tank has different surge times. When a surge occurs, it spreads across the tank over a few seconds.

A tanker may experience a side-to-side surge that may be dangerous for the driver. Hence, when loading bulkhead tanks, it is recommended that you spread the weight evenly among the tanks rather than loading the full weight on the rear or front tanks.

3. **Surge**

A surge problem occurs when the liquid carried in a tank moves around. This is a huge problem that tanker drivers must contend with.

Surge is common when a tanker stops. As the liquid moves forward and hits the front of the tank, it has a corresponding impact on the truck and shoves it forward. The tank experiences an opposite reaction when the liquid moves backward and hits the back of the tank.

The danger is that during a surge, a tanker can be shoved into a stationary vehicle. When advancing towards an intersection, a tanker may be shoved forward as a vehicle stops. Thus, running into an intersection unexpectedly can have dire consequences for a vehicle and driver.

Another area where surge is more pronounced is when trying to stop a vehicle on ice. The tank may experience a series of side-to-side surges that can eventually trigger rollover if not properly handled.

4. **Outage**

Heating a liquid causes its expansion. When the contents of a tank are warm, the contents may overflow once they expand, especially if it's a full tank. Overflowing liquid on a tarred road may cause skidding and rollover. Thus, when loading your tank, leave some room (outage) at the top of the tank to accommodate for such expansion.

When transporting a liquid in your tank, know its expansion rate so you know the right outage to leave during loading to prevent spillover. Remember that different liquids have different expansion rates.

5. Baffles and Smooth Bore Tanks

Some tanks have baffles. These are internal structures in the tanks with some holes. Although they are somewhat similar to bulkheads, baffles are only internal structures and don't actually serve as dividers for tanks.

When surging occurs in a tank, it goes around and through the baffles. This can have a huge impact on surge duration and decreases the impact of surging on the driving. Baffles are thus necessary in tanks for their ability to control unnecessary surge that can have a damaging effect on a tank.

Another group of tanks is smooth bore tanks. These don't have internal partitions and thus can't reduce surge, unlike baffles.

These tank types are specifically used for transporting foods and food products. It is a requirement in most states that tankers that are used for transporting food products must have smooth bore tanks.

Thus, they are used for hauling fruit juice, milk, drinking water, wine, etc. When hauling food and related products with smooth bore tanks, you must be extremely careful and pay attention to the following safety precautions.

Tanker Driving Precautions

Driving a tanker requires some level of experience. In addition to your level of experience, obeying some general driving precautions while behind the wheel will guarantee your safety:

1. Change lanes slowly and carefully.
2. When stopping, don't release your brakes too early.
3. Don't follow other vehicles too closely. Allow some distance between you and other vehicles to make it easier for you to avoid running into them if they stop abruptly. Know the appropriate amount of space you need to stop and factor that into your driving, especially when stopping the vehicle.
4. Create room for surge and envisage its forward impact.
5. Use stag or controlled braking for a quick stop when necessary.
6. When applying brakes, keep the pressure on the brakes steady.
7. Be aware that quick steering is dangerous. It increases the risk of rolling over.

8. When approaching curves, slow down. However, when driving through the curve, accelerate slightly.
9. When driving around corners, you may see speed limits posted around the corners. These are meant for cars only. As a tank driver, you should drive at a speed far lower than the posted speed limits.
10. Take extra precautions when driving on wet roads. As you must slow down when approaching corners, you should do the same on wet roads. It is advisable that you double the stopping distance on such roads. Remember that you can stop a loaded vehicle faster than an empty one.
11. If you wear sunglasses, remove them when you are entering a tunnel. Be prepared for a gust of wind when you are exiting the tunnel.
12. If tanks are leaking, fix them before driving the tanker. You run the risk of being fined or shut down if you are caught driving a tanker with leaking tanks. Sometimes, you may be fined with both penalties. If there are spills from your leaking tank, you may be responsible for cleanup.
13. Don't drive a tanker with manhole covers or open valves.

Causes of Tanker Skidding

Skidding refers to when a tire slips, affecting how the vehicle is handled.

Skidding is caused in tankers by several factors. These include:

- Over-accelerating.
- Quick steering.
- Excessive braking.

If any of these factors cause your vehicle to skid, take corrective action immediately:

- Release the brake immediately. This step restores traction.
- Apply the brakes again to make it easier to control the vehicle.

Tanker Inspection Procedure

A thorough inspection of your vehicle is important. Heavy vehicles require a special inspection that covers their numerous parts. Thus, it is advisable that you consult the manufacturer's manual when inspecting your tanker.

Always check the following parts for leaks:

- Everywhere under the vehicle.
- The vents should be clear and not leaking.
- Check the tires for leaking and/or wear. The tire spray is another place you should check.

- Check the manhole covers. They should be closed and sealed or latched.
- Check that all the ports and covers have gaskets and are easy to close.
- Ensure the hoses are in good condition and are stored correctly.
- Check the cut-off valves and discharge/intake ports and ensure that they are in good condition.
- Check the tank body for leaks and dents.

Must-Have Special Purpose Equipment

For ease and convenience of use, some tanker manufacturers equip their brands with some special purpose equipment. Some of this may include:

- Grounding or bonding cables for connecting the chassis and engine block together. They are ideal for grounding electrical accessories to the engine block rather than to the chassis.
- Built-in fire extinguishers.
- Vapor recovery kits. They are used for preventing gasoline vapor from escaping into the atmosphere. The goal is to reduce pollution and potentially explosive fumes.

For increased safety, you may need some additional equipment such as eye protection, gloves and hard hats.

Familiarize yourself with the most important safety and fire equipment for your vehicle and always include it in your tool kit.

Chapter Six: Passenger Transport

A passenger vehicle transports a minimum of 16 passengers, including the driver. You can't drive such a vehicle in the United States without a CDL passenger endorsement, otherwise known as a P Endorsement.

This endorsement allows you to drive passenger vehicles such as motor coaches, livery vehicles and public service vehicles. The endorsement also covers taxis, buses, service buses for factories, church buses, airport shuttles and limousines.

As with other endorsements, you must pass a basic skills and knowledge test. In this case it's the CDL Passenger Test and the CDL General Knowledge Test. If your passenger vehicle is equipped with air brakes, you must also pass the corresponding Air Brakes Endorsement Test.

The P Endorsement test will cover the following topics:

Use of Emergency Exits

The driver of a commercial passenger bus is expected to be knowledgeable about the operations and use of emergency exits.

These exits can be used to evacuate a passenger bus during emergencies such as a crash, a fire and other unfortunate events that may jeopardize the lives of both the driver and the passengers.

Understandably, there is usually a stampede and chaos during an emergency. This may lead to injuries, and sometimes, to loss of life. Thus, it is important that a passenger driver understand exit procedures and is able to lead an orderly evacuation to ensure passengers' safety.

By utilizing both special exits and regular exits, a driver can easily evacuate passengers. The emergency exits provide an alternative escape route if the regular exits are blocked.

One of the most important things you must know is the right time to conduct an evacuation. In situations such as a fire, for instance, you are expected to act swiftly in order to safeguard the lives of your passengers.

Other situations may require you to consider alternatives to evacuation. A typical example is a collision that doesn't lead to serious injuries or loss of life. In such a situation, it may be advisable to wait for law enforcement agents before evacuating the bus.

According to the FMSCA, drivers should test their emergency exits every 90 days. They are required to record their results and have an inspector sign that record.

When transporting passengers, inform them of all the emergency exits in your vehicle. Ensure the exits are all clearly labeled. Your explanation should include how such exits are used and other related safety tips.

In an emergency, make sure you:

- Inform your passenger of the need to evacuate everyone without delay. This will allay their fears. On the other hand, if you leave them in the dark, that may frighten them and cause problems.
- Conduct a row-by-row evacuation. This ensures that you account for any missing person.
- Alternate evacuating sides of the bus.
- Direct the passengers to a safe place where they can all be accounted for after the evacuation is complete. Thus, before the evacuation begins, survey your environment and look at places where passengers can stand safely until help arrives.
- Don't operate a passenger bus with the emergency exit locked if there are passengers aboard.
- Ensure that the exit is easily accessible from inside. The only exception to this is when you are operating a passenger vehicle transporting people in police custody or if you are contracted by law enforcement agencies.

Note that passenger vehicles don't share the same structure as other commercial vehicles. Hence, you are required to pass both a practical driving test and a written test. Once you are done with the written test, you can proceed to the test center for the skills test.

Passenger Transport License Requirements

The requirements are:

- You must be at least 21 years old.
- You must have a minimum of three years of driving experience.

You are not eligible to take the test and obtain the endorsement if:

- You have previously been convicted of driving under the influence.

- You have previously been convicted of serious crimes such as arson, kidnapping and acts of terrorism.

You will undergo a test that will test your knowledge in the following areas:

Passenger Transport Prohibited Practices
As a driver, you should *not*:

- Talk with passengers or engage in other distracting activities while driving. Being distracted while you are behind the wheel is dangerous and can lead to a fatal accident. If you must address the passengers, pull over.
- Fuel your bus while passengers are on board. The vapor emitted by fuel can be hazardous if inhaled.

After-Trip Vehicle Inspection
At the end of each completed trip, inspect your vehicle, paying attention to the inside. Check the windows, seats, handholds, emergency exits and other areas which riders may damage, either intentionally or accidentally.

If you are an interstate carrier, a written inspection report must be completed after each trip and submitted to your employer. In the report, specify the type of bus you drive and the identified damages so that they can be repaired.

The brake-door interlock is an essential component of a passenger bus that a driver should master due to its efficiency and associated benefits. Most transit buses are equipped with this important device, designed to prevent the vehicle from moving while passengers are alighting from it.

When the passenger bus comes to a complete stop, the door interlocks are automatically engaged. Once the doors are closed, the interlocks will disengage automatically. Thus, it functions as a secondary parking brake. Even so, the interlock is not a replacement for the parking brake. While it complements the efforts of the parking brake, some drivers erroneously replace the brake with the interlock. They simply take their foot off the brake pad, leaving only the interlock to stop and hold the vehicle. That can be dangerous and lead to a crash.

Passenger Transport Inspection Procedure
As a public passenger bus driver, always inspect your vehicle before you leave for work each day. You should routinely inspect the following areas:

1. **Engine Compartment**

- Check the oil level. Operating your vehicle when it's obviously short of engine oil can be disastrous. Make sure the oil is at a safe level, usually between "Add" and "Full."
- Check the power steering. The level should be between "Add" and "Full." It must not be leaking and should be securely mounted.
- Check the water pump. Pay attention to the bolts. Are they tight enough and securely mounted?
- Check the alternator. Are the bolts tight and securely mounted? What about the belt? It shouldn't be frayed or cracked. It should maintain a tension between ½" and ¾".
- Check the air compressor. You don't want to risk running out of air pressure when you need it most. The belt should be in good order. If it's cracked, or frayed, it needs urgent attention. The hoses should be tightly secured, same as the bolts.

2. **Under the Vehicle**

Pay attention to the following parts:

- **Exhaust system:** Check for signs of leaking exhaust. Also check the clamps to ensure they're tight.
- **Driveshaft:** A driveshaft is a mechanical device that is used for connecting the components of a drive train that cannot be directly connected due to distance issues in a large vehicle. The shaft crack shouldn't have any cracks. The bolts must be tight. Check for signs of cracks and holes. If you find any, fix them without delay.

  Some other signs of a bad shaft include intense vibration that can be felt underneath the vehicle.

  Another problem common to the driveshaft is abnormal noise. This may arise when the supportive bearing or bushing for the driveshaft U-joints or the driveshaft itself fails or wears out. The result is usually clunking, rattling, squeaking or scraping.

  Other problems are shuddering while accelerating and turning. The former is usually caused by a bad center bearing or a loose U-joint within the driveshaft while the latter is the result of a broken or bad driveshaft that can prevent the wheels from turning properly.

  A driveshaft is also referred to as tailshaft, propeller shaft, driving shaft and Cardan shaft.

- **Frame:** The frame should be checked for cracks. Check the bolts for tightness. Loose bolts are an indication that something is wrong with the frame and it needs urgent attention.

3. **General Check**

Other important parts of the vehicle you should check are:

- The parking brake. Apply the brakes and put the truck in low gear. Try to move the vehicle. Does it move or not?
- Check the service brake. Pull the vehicle forward at five miles/hour. Then, stop the vehicle by applying the brakes and observe if there is a pull right or pull left effect.
- The windshield should be inspected too. It must be clean without cracks, obstructive stickers or chips. This extends to the mirrors too. They must be properly adjusted, clean and sticker-free.

4. **Safety/Emergency Equipment**

Check the following:

- Spare breakers or fuses. This depends on what your vehicle is equipped with. These fuses or breakers are used as replacements if the original fuse or breaker is blown.
- Fire extinguisher. It must be mounted and fully charged. If you don't have one, buy it immediately. You never can tell, a fire extinguisher can make a difference between the total destruction of your vehicle by fire and being able to put out the fire with minimal damage.
- Three triangles. This is a set of three triangles you can put on the side of the road to warn other road users of a crash or breakdown ahead. This is necessary safety equipment you should always have in your toolbox. Choose the red, reflective type so they're most useful at night.

This is just a handful of some parts of the vehicle you should include in your pre-trip inspection. Transporting passengers with a malfunctioning vehicle can be risky. A routine inspection of the necessary parts of the vehicle can help you to avoid that and make the roads safer.

Passenger Bus Safety Tips

You can complement the pre-trip inspection by implementing these safety tips:

1. Keep the aisles clear. Obstacles in the aisle can impede movement and/or cause tripping, which could lead to injuries.

2. While driving in the No-Zone, watch out for other vehicles. Some drivers may be oblivious to your bus' size. These are blind spots around buses or danger areas where the likelihood of crashes is pretty high.
3. When approaching work areas or construction sites, slow down considerably. Large vehicles frequent such sites and you may run into them if you don't drive at a safe speed.

4. Drive defensively at all times. Aggressive driving is reportedly responsible for two-thirds of traffic fatalities across the United States. Hence, it is advisable to maintain a safe speed and keep your distance.
5. Fasten your seat belt. The seat belt increases your safety behind the wheel as in the event of a crash, it will reduce the impact and can thus save your life and that of your passengers or fellow road users.
6. Don't allow passengers to leave their carry-on baggage in the doorway. Baggage should be placed so as not to obstruct any place in the vehicle, including the exits and the entrance.
7. While buses are permitted to carry small arms ammunition that is clearly labeled ORM-D, along with drugs and emergency hospital supplies, you may not transport liquid Class 6 poisons such as cresols, lead compounds, cyanides, biological samples, some pesticides, clinical waste, irritating substances or division 2.3 gas that is known to be toxic to humans.

   You mustn't carry over 100 pounds of solid Class 6 poisons and explosives in spaces that are designed to be occupied by people. Under no condition should you carry labeled radioactive materials in seats meant for passengers.
8. Passenger bus drivers are forbidden from transporting animals. The exception is service animals. A physically challenged passenger with signal dog(s) can also be allowed into a vehicle alongside the dog(s).
9. Don't allow passengers on the bus until around the departure time. This is an effective way to prevent vandalism.

Driving a passenger bus can be both challenging and rewarding. Having a comprehensive knowledge of the rules and equipment will make your job that much easier.

Chapter Seven: School Bus Endorsement

US federal regulations make it mandatory for drivers who operate school buses to obtain a School Bus Endorsement.

To become a school bus driver, you must undergo a full training program that includes the following:

- Understanding the state rules and regulations guiding school bus driving.
- Practical instructions about school bus driving. This includes instructions about handling the vehicle and its maintenance.
- Customer service skills. Dealing with students from different backgrounds has its challenges. You must be trained and experienced enough to manage students with their different requests, actions and complaints

School Bus Driver's License Endorsement Requirements

To get a school bus endorsement, you must:

- Be at least 21 years old.
- Have a minimum of three years of driving experience.
- Pass the CDL endorsement and knowledge test.
- Take and pass a road test in the type of school bus you wish to drive.
- Have a perfect driving record. Your driving history may work against you, especially if there are question marks.
- Meet hearing and vision requirements. Communication is one of the keys to your success as a driver. Hearing and good vision are important for this.
- Be physically and morally fit.
- Submit a fully completed Medical Examiner's Certificate from the federal government. This is in addition to a copy of a Medical Examiner's Certificate you must submit every two years. In some cases, your physician will determine the frequency with which this certificate must be submitted.

  The objective is to ensure that you have both the physical and mental capacity to handle the challenges associated with driving a school bus.

The test will cover the following:

1. **School Bus Loading and Unloading**

Most accidents involving school buses occur during the loading and unloading stages. According to some sources, such as the Kansas Department of Transportation, pupils are more vulnerable to injuries and fatalities while getting on or off school buses.

The source cited data from 2005 to 2006. Within that period, some 13 K-2 children were involved in fatal accidents. This figure is more than the number of students that were actually killed inside a school bus. It shows a disturbing trend: getting off or on a school bus is more challenging than most people generally consider it to be.

The high rate of fatalities during the loading and offloading area explains the rationale behind the area being referred to as the "danger zone."

Specifically, the "danger zone" refers to parts of the vehicle where passengers are more vulnerable to accidents. These are areas where the driver's vision is blurred so he/she may not be able to see the boarding or exiting students clearly. Such areas include 10 feet on either side of the vehicle, in front of the vehicle and behind.

To curb the accidents, the National Safety Council, through the School Transportation Section, recommends special training for drivers to increase their effectiveness and overall competence in operating school buses.

Each state is encouraged to adapt the endorsement exam as appropriate for its needs.

Typical topics covered on the exam include:

- Drivers must approach the loading and unloading areas slowly and carefully.
- Drivers should activate flashing warning lights before making a stop. The recommended distance is 100 feet before the stop zone.
- Loading and unloading should be done in designated places only. Picking up or dropping off students at undesignated drop-off and pick-up points is criminal and exposes the students to accidents and injuries.
- Pupils shouldn't be allowed to cross the road behind the school bus since it's a blind spot.
- Before you leave the drop-off or pick-up point, double-check all side mirrors and crossovers for traffic or students. Leave only when the coast is clear.
- Examine your stops regularly. If you see unsafe conditions, promptly report them to the supervisor.
- After completing a route, take a walk through the bus. Check for acts of vandalism, sleeping students and forgotten articles. Make sure that everyone is off the vehicle before moving. Report noticeable acts of vandalism to the school management. Take forgotten articles to the appropriate place.
- Before you open the door for loading or unloading, put the vehicle in neutral. Use the parking brake as well to ensure the vehicle is fully stopped.
- Before you move your vehicle after loading or unloading, listen and look for signs that a vehicle or student may be near your bus. To enhance your hearing, it is

advisable that you silence passengers and turn off radios and other noisy equipment to enable you to hear better.

- Before you allow pupils to exit or approach the bus, make sure that the flow of traffic on both sides has been stopped.
- Don't move the school bus until the students inside the school bus are properly seated or those outside the bus are at a safe distance.
- Jacket straps or strings, book bags, clothing and backpacks can become entangled in the school bus' doorway. This is one of the leading causes of accidents in school buses. Pay attention to the students as they are exiting or boarding your bus. This will enable you to ensure they are safe or to provide the necessary assistance that can prevent such an incident.
- At the beginning of a school season, give the students practical tips that will ensure smooth and safe loading and unloading procedures.
- Teach the students signals that will notify them of potential dangers and suggest practical steps they can take to avoid such problems. For instance, if you honk the horn twice, it should convey a message. A different message should be conveyed when you honk three times.
- Don't pick students up at corners shortly before you make a right turn. It is safer to unload them after turning. You have no idea of what is going on around the corner.

2. Passenger Bus Post-Trip Inspection

After each trip, conduct a post-trip inspection. Move around the bus and through it. Look for:

- Sleeping students. If you find sleeping students, wake them up immediately. Make sure that everyone has left the vehicle before you end your workday.
- Articles accidentally left behind on the bus.
- Damage. Report any act of vandalism to the school management or the appropriate authority
- Any open doors and windows.
- Operational or mechanical problems on the bus. Pay attention to flashing warning lamps, mirror systems and stop signal arms.

If you notice any problem with any of these during the inspection, notify the school authorities or your supervisor immediately.

How to Plan for Emergencies

When you are faced with emergencies, your response will determine their impact on you, the vehicle and/or the students.

Firstly, recognize the problem. If you have enough time, notify your dispatcher and explain the problem before deciding whether to evacuate the bus or not.

If you are contemplating emptying the bus, consider these factors:

- Are the students at risk of greater danger if they remain in the school bus?
- Would removing them expose them to severe weather or speeding traffic?
- What are the probabilities that the vehicle may be hit by another vehicle?
- Will moving the students complicate back and neck injuries or fractures?

Evacuation is mandatory under the following conditions:

- The bus is adjacent to or stalled on a railroad-highway crossing.
- The possibility of an accident is high.
- There is a threat of a fire or the bus is already on fire.
- A hazardous material spills, constituting an imminent threat to life.
- The bus may change position, thereby increasing the danger students are exposed to.

Standard Evacuation Procedures

Evacuation may be mandatory during an accident or life-threatening event. As soon as possible, start planning ahead for emergencies that may demand student evacuation. Assign responsible and older student assistants to each of the emergency exits. Teach these students the best way to assist others during a crisis.

This can sometimes be easier said than done, especially if there are no older students to assist you when an emergency situation arises. This underscores the importance of keeping everyone on the same page as you, security wise.

Explain the evacuation procedures to everyone on your bus. They should be knowledgeable about how to operate the emergency exits. Teach them the importance of following instructions during an emergency. Such advanced planning will make a huge difference when handling emergencies.

To keep students safe outside the bus during an emergency:

- If there is a fire or a threat of imminent fire, take the students upwind. One hundred feet away from the bus, in the direction of oncoming vehicles, is a safe place.
- If students are at risk due to spilled hazardous materials, lead them upwind of the bus, at least 300 feet away.

- If you are close to railroad tracks, lead the students away from the tracks as far as possible in the direction of oncoming trains.

The General Procedures

This is a summary of the general evacuation procedure

- First determine the most practical type of evacuation. Sometimes, you may have to combine more than one evacuation method.
- Secure the vehicle. Place it in neutral or park. Set the parking brakes and shut the engine off. Remove the ignition key and activate the hazard lights. If you have enough time, inform your dispatch office of the development. Notify them of your condition, location and the assistance you need.
- Ask passing motorists or pedestrians for help. If that is not possible, assign two responsible students to go and ask for help.
- Evacuate without delay. If there are students with neck or head injuries, if at all possible don't move them until professionals are on hand to do that.
- Assign a responsible and older student to lead other students to a safe place.
- Once they have alighted from the bus, walk through to ensure that all students have been successfully evacuated.
- Account for all students.
- Protect the area and set out necessary emergency warning devices to warn other road users of potential danger.
- Prepare information in advance for emergency responders.

Passenger Bus Accident Management Tips

The possibility of an accident involving your bus can't be ruled out. Since you can't control other drivers or road users, accidents will happen.

A school bus driver should understand the best accident management procedure to minimize the impact of the accident and ensure the overall safety of the passengers.

You must report an accident as soon as possible, starting with the transportation bus stop first. Do this via radio and provide the department with the following information:

- Location of the accident.
- Number of students involved.
- Number of vehicles involved.
- Number of injured students.

After contacting the transportation bus stop, take the following steps:

- Keep all the students on the bus for safety reasons. Conversely, if appropriate, remove students without delay.
- Once the students are off the bus, keep them together. Supervise them and ensure that they don't wander off.
- Don't release students to parents, neighbors or other family members.
- Don't allow the students to walk home or leave the scene.
- Keep the students as calm as possible.
- If the students are to be transferred to another bus, prepare them for the transfer.

Student Evacuation Procedure

To ensure a smooth student evacuation:

- Call the bus dispatch first.
- Secure the school bus by setting the brake, shutting off the motor and removing the keys.
- Choose a safe place to assemble outside the bus at a reasonable distance from danger.
- Determine the safest and most appropriate evacuation method and route. Your options include side doors, the roof hatch, front door, windows or rear exit. If any of these aren't appropriate for the evacuation, you can kick out the rear glass panels and windshield.
- If you are running out of time, ask students to leave their personal belongings in the vehicle to make the evacuation faster.
- Check the floor area and seats to ensure that the vehicle is completely empty.
- Steer clear of the bus until it is declared fit for use by the appropriate authorities or by bus dispatch.
- Follow the Student Release and Accountability procedures.
- You should only leave the bus after making sure that all students have been evacuated from it.
- Stay with the students to calm their nerves and assure them of their safety.

Sometimes, emergencies are caused by inclement weather. If your emergency is caused by poor visibility, you must evacuate the students to a safe area as soon as possible. The poor visibility may have the same impact on other drivers too, leading to a collision with your vehicle. Hence, a swift evacuation is of paramount importance.

School Lockdown Procedures

When there is a threat to a school's staff, students or faculty members, the school will respond with a lockdown.

The lockdown does not allow people to exit or enter the school until the threat is averted. Some situations that may require a school lockdown include:

- Riots.
- Shooting.
- Hostage situations.
- Natural disasters.
- Police activity in the neighborhood.
- Medical emergencies.
- Internal threats.

Sometimes, during a school lockdown, it may be necessary for you to ensure the safety of students on your bus.

There are two types of lockdown:

1. **Code Red**

A Code Red Lockdown is for emergency situations that involve a serious threat to life such as an active shooter that may require students to hide or take a protective cover.

In such a situation, take these protective actions:

- Decide whether to stay put or drive the bus and passengers away from the danger.
- Secure the vehicle's door immediately.
- Announce a Code Red Lockdown and order the students to get down away from windows. Instruct them to be quiet and remain hidden.
- When it is safe to do so, contact bus dispatch.
- Don't release any students or allow anyone into the bus after the lockdown order.
- Periodically, reassure the students of their safety.
- As the situation changes, reevaluate safety measures and act accordingly.

2. **Code Yellow**

Sometimes, an emergency situation may be such that students are safer on the bus than being evacuated. Such a situation triggers a Code Yellow Lockdown. A typical example of such situations includes blocked roads, some medical emergencies, landslides, weather-related emergencies and traffic jams.

If you are transporting students during a Code Yellow Lockdown:

- Contact bus dispatch for immediate assistance.
- Park in a safe place.

- If students must stay in the place beyond your original plans, inform the students of the change of plans.
- Don't allow them to leave the bus and consistently reassure them of their safety.
- Follow the Student Accountability and Release security procedures.

When you are faced with either a Code Red or a Code Yellow Lockdown, you can choose to stick to these instructions or deviate from them, depending on the situation. Do whatever is necessary to safeguard students.

3. Shelter-In-Place

A shelter-in-place situation may arise when the environment is contaminated with hazardous materials.

You may either drive the vehicle away from the contaminated environment or seal off the bus completely, depending on the situation on the ground.

Follow the procedures below if you notice hazardous materials close to your bus:

- Call bus dispatch without delay.
- Close all the doors and windows.
- If there are outside vents on the bus, close them.
- Turn off all ventilation or heating systems.
- Move the bus away from the hazardous waste. Go upwind and uphill from the contaminant, if possible.
- If necessary, follow existing evacuation procedures.
- If any students exhibit symptoms such as fainting, shortness of breath, headache, dizziness or unexplained coughing, request medical attention as soon as possible.

4. Code Green

A Code Green Lockdown occurs when a situation requires that staff and students move to a new location or outdoors. Such a situation may include a gas leak or a bomb threat.

The evacuation may require the transportation of students and staff to a new location with the school bus.

Mechanical Troubles

Mechanical troubles may arise when you least expect. Depending on the location and type of mechanical issues, you must take practical steps to ensure that your passengers are safe.

If your bus develops mechanical problems, do the following:

- If possible, drive the vehicle to a safe place before stopping it. Once it stops, secure it and put the four-way flashers on.
- Decide to leave the students in the vehicle or evacuate them after considering all the factors impacting their safety.
- Implement a Code Yellow Lockdown or an evacuation order and follow appropriate procedures.
- Reassure the students of their safety and remain calm and in control of the situation.
- Put out warning triangles, especially if you are on a blind corner to warn other drivers of a problem and prevent them from running into your vehicle.
- Account for the students and supervise them. Under no circumstance should you release the students to go home on their own. The Student Accountability and Release procedures are to guide you.
- Never leave the students without adult supervision.
- If necessary, follow existing Transfer Procedures.

<u>ABS for School Buses</u>

School buses that weigh over 10,000 pounds are mandated to have the Antilock Brake System (ABS).

The ABS in a school bus has the following components:

- Wheel speed sensors: The wheel speed sensor, also known as the vehicle speed sensor, is a device with a pickup and toothed ring that is used to read the speed at which a vehicle's wheels rotate.
- An electronic controller: This component is designed to minimize skidding while helping the driver to maintain steering control even in extremely difficult braking conditions. It uses the wheel speed sensors to analyze the speed in all the vehicle's wheels and compare them. It can also recognize wheel speed changes at the speed of light. Thus, it can detect an impending skid with ease, allowing the modulator to adjust the application pressure in the brake. It can make about 40 adjustments each second.

Note that the efficiency of the braking system depends on how you use it. You must pay constant attention to the vehicle's ABS dash indicator light that is designed to alert drivers of a malfunction.

If you receive a warning signal from the indicator, inspect both the electrical and wiring connectors in the vehicle. Follow manufacturer recommendations to correct the issue. Otherwise, contact a professional technician to fix the braking problem.

Student Management

Student management is an integral part of your job description. Loading and unloading students can be challenging. Nevertheless, for their safety, you must concentrate on your driving regardless of what is going on in the vehicle.

If there are serious issues that need urgent attention, you are advised to stop the vehicle and attend to them.

These are some problem-solving tips you can implement when handling serious problems:

- If you see the need to discipline problematic students, do that strictly according to school procedure.
- Stop the vehicle when necessary and park in a driveway, a parking lot or any other safe location.
- Secure the vehicle and address the offender(s) respectively. While addressing them, be firm without being rude or angry.
- If you can solve the problem with a change of seating, move the student to another place. A seat very close to you is best.
- Regardless of what happens on the vehicle, don't kick any student off the bus except at the designated bus stop or school.
- If the issue is beyond your control and may compromise your driving, notify the school. Alternatively, call the police to address the issue.

School Bus Special Safety Skills

While driving, you should also pay attention to some special safety considerations that will increase students' safety. Some areas that deserve a special mention are:

1. When Driving in High Winds

Driving in high winds can affect how you handle a school bus and can be very dangerous. They may push the school bus around or move it off the road. In some extreme conditions, a rollover or tip-over is a possibility.

When driving in high winds, take the following precautions for increased safety:

- Grip the steering wheel firmly. Gusts are possible, so anticipate them.

- Slow down or pull off the road. This will reduce the huge impact of the wind on your vehicle considerably.
- If you need more information, contact your dispatcher.

2. **Using Strobe Lights**

If your school bus is equipped with white strobe lights, you should use the roof-mounted light when struggling with limited visibility.

3. **Backing Up**

School bus drivers are not encouraged to back up unless there are no better ways to move the bus. You should also remember not to back up a bus when students are outside it.

However, if backing up your bus is the only way out, follow the tips discussed earlier in the book. Before you reverse, make sure that all your students are on the bus.

School Bus Inspection

You should inspect your school bus before every trip.

Check the following parts during the inspection:

- Hoses: When checking the hoses, look for leaking fluids beneath the transmission and engine. These could indicate a hose is leaking. Puddles are also an indication of a leaking pipe.
- Oil levels: Don't ever drive a vehicle without checking the oil level. If it is above the refill mark, it is within a safe operating range. Otherwise, don't drive the vehicle until you refill the oil.
- Temperature gauge: Inspect the gauge and ensure that it works normally. The temperature light shouldn't be on. When the bus is turned on the gauge should start climbing to the normal operating range.
- Mirrors and windshield: The mirrors must be clean and properly adjusted before every trip.
  The windshield should also be clean and unobstructed by things such as stickers.
- Lights/reflectors: When checking these components, pay attention to the following:
  - Backing lights.
  - Clearance lights.
  - Brake lights.
  - Taillights.
  - Headlights.
  - Strobe light.

    - Red reflectors and amber reflectors, on the rear and elsewhere respectively.
- Check the emergency kit to ensure it contains spare electrical fuses (if your vehicle requires them), a fire extinguisher and three red reflective triangles.
- Inspect the body fluid cleanup kit to ensure it is in good condition.
- Check the external and internal mirrors for proper adjustment and cleanliness. You should also inspect the mirrors and their brackets for signs of poor mounting or damage.
- Check the right turn signal, the left turn signal, your Antilock Braking System indicator, the four-way emergency flashers and the high-beam headlight.
- Check the tires too. When checking the tires, pay attention to the following:
    - Tire condition: Are the sidewalls or tread in good condition? Check the stems and valve caps as well.
    - Tread depth: If you are using steering axle tires, a depth of 4/32 is okay. On other tires, 2/32 is the acceptable tire depth.
    - Tire inflation: Use a tire gauge to check the inflation.
- Check the emergency exits and make sure they operate smoothly and can be closed securely from anywhere, including inside. Inspect the emergency exit warning devices to ensure they're in good condition.
- Check the entry door to ensure it opens and closes smoothly.
  Check the handrails. The step light should be in good condition and the handrails should be firmly secured.
- If the school bus is equipped with a handicap lift, check it for damaged, leaking or missing parts. The lift must be latched securely and should retract with ease. If there are problems, notify the appropriate authorities immediately.

Railroad Crossing Procedures

Annually, some 4,000 collisions result in about 1,100 injuries and 400 fatalities at railroad crossings across the United States. These statistics include school buses and students. To prevent such occurrences, the National Safety Council recommends specific safety procedures for all school bus drivers:

1. Pay careful attention to traffic when stopping at railroad crossings. Check for incoming and oncoming vehicles and make appropriate provisions for them. When preparing to stop, tap the brakes to warn other drivers. Always use the school bus hazard lights.
2. Before crossing the tracks, make sure that you stop the bus completely whether you are carrying passengers or not. It is advisable that you stop the bus between 15 and 50 feet from the railroad tracks.
3. If you are driving on multiple-lane roads, don't make a turn after crossing the tracks unless it is absolutely necessary.

4. As soon as you stop the vehicle before the crossing, open the driver's window and service door. Turn off noisy equipment such as fans and radios. Ask the students to keep quiet while you listen and look in both directions for approaching trains.
5. Under no condition should you cross the tracks until you have a clear view of the tracks and are convinced that the coast is clear without any approaching trains.
6. If a train is passing from one direction, don't assume that the other side is clear. Another train may be hidden somewhere and may be approaching from another track. Wait until the train passes and the tracks are clear before crossing.
7. Don't ignore railroad crossing signals. Watch out for warning devices such as bells or gates and obey such signals. Obey flagmen or police officers if they are manning the tracks and give you specific instructions about crossing. That doesn't imply that you should blindly cross the tracks, though. Even when following their instructions, confirm that there are no approaching trains before crossing.
8. If your vehicle gets stuck on the tracks while crossing, evacuate the students immediately. Move them a safe distance away from the tracks and notify the dispatcher of your situation. If you sight an approaching train, have the students walk at a 45-degree angle away from the tracks in the direction of the approaching train.
9. If weather conditions such as snow, fog, wind and rain affect both your hearing and your visibility, exercise extra caution when crossing railroad tracks.
10. If you spot malfunctioning railroad signals, report them to the school transportation department or personnel.

If you pass the CDL test and qualify for the endorsement, your Road Test Evaluation Form (CDL-200) will be returned to you as proof that you successfully passed the exam. To receive your endorsement, visit the DMV and turn in the form no more than seven days after passing the test.

<u>What if You Fail the Test?</u>

Some drivers pass the test on the first attempt. Others may have to retake the exam.

You can retake the test within a couple of days or at your convenience. If you fail the first retest, you can take the test again after waiting for at least 90 days during which it's assumed you'll improve your knowledge and skills.

Generally, your permit allows you to retake the test three times. If you fail the three attempts, you must obtain another permit to enable you to take the exam again.

Note that some states allow applicants to only retake the part of the test they fail. Nevertheless, if you fail three times, you will have to take the whole test over again.

To be eligible to retest:

- You must have a valid driver's license or learner's permit.
- You mustn't have other road tests scheduled as of the time of the payment.
- You must provide your DMV ID Number. You can get this from the Client ID Number or your learner's permit.
- You must provide your date of birth as proof of your age, one of the major eligibility requirements.

If you meet the requirements, you can then pay for the additional tests using a debit or credit card.

General Knowledge Test 1 – 50 questions

1. A driver who is transporting property is allowed to:
    a. Drive 12 hours at most after being off for 10 consecutive hours.
    b. Drive 11 hours at most after being off for 10 consecutive hours.
    c. Drive 10 hours at most after being off for 10 consecutive hours.
    d. Drive 9 hours at most after being off for 10 consecutive hours.

2. A driver who is carrying passengers is allowed to:
    a. Drive 12 hours at most after being off for 8 consecutive hours.
    b. Drive 11 hours at most after being off for 8 consecutive hours.
    c. Drive 10 hours at most after being off for 8 consecutive hours.
    d. Drive 9 hours at most after being off for 8 consecutive hours.

3. A driver who is carrying passengers is allowed to drive a maximum of:
    a. 60/70 hours within a time frame of 7/8 consecutive days.
    b. 65/75 hours within a time frame of 7/8 consecutive days.
    c. 70/80 hours within a time frame of 7/8 consecutive days.
    d. 75/85 hours within a time frame of 7/8 consecutive days.

4. By law, how often are you required to complete a DOT inspection for your commercial vehicle?
    a. Every 6 months.
    b. Every 12 months.
    c. Every 8 months.
    d. Every 4 months.

5. What is a CDL?
    a. A Commercial Driver's License.
    b. A Commercial Driving License.
    c. A Community Driving License.
    d. None of the above.

6. What is CLP?
    a. Community License Producers.
    b. Commercial Learning Permit.
    c. Commercial Learner's Permit.
    d. Commercial Learner Permit.

7. Which of the following is true?
    a. CDL drivers cannot take illegal drugs but can take all legal drugs.
    b. CDL drivers can take illegal and legal drugs.
    c. CDL drivers cannot take illegal drugs and also some legal drugs are prohibited.
    d. None of the above.

8. A driver may be disqualified to operate a commercial vehicle under DOT regulations if the following substance is found to be taken by the driver.
    a. Cocaine.
    b. Oxycodone.
    c. Codeine.
    d. All of the above.

9. Drivers must submit DOT physical test results every .....
    a. 1 year.
    b. 2 years.
    c. 3 years.
    d. 4 years.

10. The restrictions on unregistered vehicles and unlicensed drivers were announced through the ...
    a. The Commercial Motor Vehicle and Driver Safety Act.
    b. The Motor Vehicle Safety Act.
    c. The Commercial Motor Vehicle Safety Act.
    d. The Motor Vehicle Safety and Licensing Act.

11. Commercial Driver's Licenses are classified into ...
    a. Two classes.
    b. Four classes.
    c. Three classes.
    d. Five classes.

12. A Class A license is for drivers who operate which types of vehicles?
    a. Two or more vehicles with a combined weight of less than 25,000 pounds.
    b. Two or more vehicles with a combined weight of over 25,000 pounds.
    c. Two or more vehicles with a combined weight of less than 26,000 pounds.
    d. Two or more vehicles with a combined weight of over 26,000 pounds.

13. A Class A driver's license can be used to drive a wide range of vehicles except:
    a. Tractor-trailers.
    b. Tank vehicles.
    c. SUVs.
    d. Flatbeds.

14. A P Endorsement allows the holder to drive a passenger vehicle that carries a minimum of ... passengers.
    a. 15 passengers
    b. 20 passengers.
    c. 16 passengers.
    d. 10 passengers.

15. What is the TSA?
    a. The Transport Security Administration.
    b. The Transport Safety and Security Administration.
    c. The Transportation Safety Administration.
    d. The Transportation Safety and Security Administration.

16. What class of vehicle does the N Endorsement cover?
    a. Tanks.
    b. Flatbeds and SUVs.
    c. School buses.
    d. Passenger buses.

17. If you want to be a school bus driver, you need the ...
    a. P Endorsement.
    b. K Endorsement.
    c. S Endorsement.
    d. Z Endorsement.

18. Which of these states doesn't allow drivers to operate triple vehicles?
    a. North Dakota.
    b. West Virginia.
    c. Delaware.
    d. New Hampshire.

19. The ... license is issued to drivers who operate commercial vehicles with a combined weight over 26,000 pounds.
    a. Class A.
    b. Class B.
    c. Class C.
    d. Class D.

20. With the appropriate endorsement, you can drive ... vehicles with a Class B license.
    a. Class D.
    b. Class A.
    c. Class F.
    d. Class C.

21. Dump trucks, segmented buses, large passenger buses and straight trucks are some of the vehicles that can be driven with a ... license.
    a. Class D.
    b. Class B.
    c. Class A.
    d. Class C.

22. The required license class for transporting hazardous materials is ...
    a. Class C.
    b. Class D.
    c. Class B.
    d. Class A.

23. A Class 3 Truck is is known as a ......
    a. Medium truck and weighs between 10,000 pounds and 14,000 pounds.
    b. Light truck and weighs between 6,000 pounds and 8,500 pounds.
    c. Light truck and weighs between 10,000 pounds and 14,000 pounds.
    d. Medium truck and weighs between 6,000 pounds and 8,500 pounds.

24. A Class 8 Truck is known as a ......
    a. Heavy truck and weighs more than 33,000 pounds
    b. Heavy truck and weights more than 26,000 pounds.
    c. Medium truck and weighs more than 26,000 pounds.
    d. Medium truck and weighs more than 24,000 pounds.

25. A driver is deemed qualified to receive a Commercial Driver's License if he/she gets a minimum score of ... on the test.
    a. 70%.
    b. 80%.
    c. 75%.
    d. 90%.

26. A Class 4 Truck is known as a ......
    a. Light truck and weighs between 10,000 pounds and 14,000 pounds.
    b. Medium truck and weighs between 14,000 pounds and 16,000 pounds.
    c. Light truck and weighs between 14,000 pounds and 16,000 pounds.
    d. Medium truck and weighs between 10,000 pounds and 14,000 pounds.

27. A Class 7 Truck is known as a ......
    a. Medium truck and weighs between 26,000 pounds and 33,000 pounds.
    b. Medium truck and weighs between 16,000 pounds and 26,000 pounds.
    c. Heavy truck and weighs between 26,000 pounds and 33,000 pounds.
    d. Heavy truck and weighs between 30,000 pounds and 33,000 pounds.

28. A Class 5 Truck is known as a ......
    a. Medium truck and weighs between 16,000 pounds and 19,500 pounds.
    b. Heavy truck and weighs between 16,000 pounds and 19,500 pounds.
    c. Light truck and weighs between 16,000 pounds and 19,500 pounds.
    d. Medium truck and weighs between 19,500 pounds and 26,000 pounds.

29. Proof of identity includes all of the following except:
    a. Credit history.
    b. A government-issued identity card.
    c. U. S. military discharge papers.
    d. A birth certificate.

30. Which of these types of documents are acceptable for identification?
    a. Photocopies and original copies of your documents.
    b. Duplicate documents and photocopies.
    c. Original documents only.
    d. Duplicate documents and original copies of your document.

31. You can prove your citizenship or permanent residency with the following:
    a. Certificate of citizenship and birth certificate.
    b. Permanent residency papers and utility bills.
    c. US passport and work permit.
    d. All of the above.

32. Other acceptable proof of residency documents are stated in the income tax return otherwise known as the ...
    a. IRS W-2 form.
    b. IRS W-1 form.
    c. IRS P-1 form.
    d. IRS P-2 form.

33. The order of name arrangement is immaterial when filling out the Commercial Driver's License application form.
    a. Yes.
    b. No.
    c. The DMV must decide.
    d. It depends on several factors.

34. A Commercial Learner's Permit holder must wait for a minimum of ... before applying for a Commercial Driver's License.
    a. Two months.
    b. Two weeks.
    c. Three days.
    d. Ten days.

35. The minimum acceptable age to obtain a driver's license in most states is ...
    a. 18 years.
    b. 21 years.
    c. 20 years.
    d. 15 years.

36. Applicants between ... are only allowed to drive on the interstate.
    a. 19 and 20.
    b. 19 and 21.
    c. 18 and 20.
    d. 15 and 19.

37. The interstate permit expires ...
    a. When you are 22 years old.
    b. When you are 30 years old.
    c. When you are 21 years old.
    d. Not for as long as you are in the driving business.

38. The minimum age requirement for interstate driving is
    a. 35 years old.
    b. 28 years old.
    c. 21 years old.
    d. There is no minimum age.

39. All of the following may disqualify you from obtaining a Commercial Driver's License except:
    a. Inability to speak or read English fluently.
    b. Failure to produce proof of identity on request.
    c. Providing an expired government-issued identity card.
    d. None of the above.

40. A disqualified driver can have the disqualification overturned after how many years?
    a. Five years.
    b. Two years.
    c. Ten years.
    d. The decision cannot be overturned.

41. Drivers who wish to operate commercial motor vehicles must have ... vision in each eye.
    a. 20/40
    b. 30/50
    c. 40/20
    d. 50/50.

42. The acceptable value for horizontal vision is ...
    a. 130 degrees or higher
    b. 140 degrees or higher.
    c. 150 degrees or higher.
    d. 100 degrees or higher.

43. You may be disqualified from taking the test if you are found with the following items at the testing center:
    a. Written notes or other materials.
    b. Electronic devices such as cell phones.
    c. Personal effects.
    d. All of the above.

44. Driving under the influence of alcohol or drugs may result in ...
    a. A year-long ban from applying for a CDL license.
    b. A five-year ban from applying for the CDL.
    c. A fine of $500.
    d. Permanent disqualification from applying for the license.

45. The acceptable blood alcohol content acceptable for driving a commercial vehicle is ...
    a. Below 0.10.
    b. Below 0.70.
    c. Below 0.04.
    d. Below 0.05.

46. If your blood alcohol content is above the acceptable value, you may be prohibited from driving for ...
    a. 30 to 60 days.
    b. 60 days to 180 days.
    c. 30 to 45 days.
    d. 60 days to life.

47. What is the penalty for committing a felony with a commercial vehicle?
    a. You may be banned for life.
    b. You will be banned for a minimum of five years.
    c. You will be banned for at least three years.
    d. You will be banned for a year.

48. If you are convicted of manufacturing or distributing drugs illegally with a commercial motor vehicle, the penalty is:
    a. A lifetime ban.
    b. A five-year ban.
    c. A six-month ban.
    d. The duration of the ban is dependent on various factors.

49. Failing to stop at an accident scene that involves your vehicle, especially if the accident leads to a loss of life or injury, may incur:
    a. A $100 fine.
    b. A $500 fine.
    c. A lifetime driving ban.
    d. A year-long driving ban.

50. The T endorsement allows you to drive the following vehicles:
    a. Double or triple trailers.
    b. Double trailers only.
    c. Triple trailers only.
    d. None of the above.

General Knowledge Test 1 Answers

1. The correct answer is: (B). Drive 11 hours at most after being off for 10 consecutive hours.

The Federal Motor Carrier Safety Administration (Part of the Department of Transportation) has set the limit as federal law.

2. The correct answer is: (C). Drive 10 hours at most after being off for 8 consecutive hours.

The Federal Motor Carrier Safety Administration (Part of the Department of Transportation) has set the limit as federal law.

3. The correct answer is: (A). 60/70 hours within a time frame of 7/8 consecutive days.

The limit is set by the Department of Transportaion so that drivers do not burn themselves out.

4. The correct answer is: (B). Every 12 months.

This regulation is set up to ensure the safety of drivers and the public. The inspector must be a qualified person.

5. The correct answer is: (A). A Commercial Driver's License.

CDL means Commercial Driver's License. This is a type of license that is issued to drivers who wish to operate commercial vehicles. The wide range of commercial vehicles that a holder of this license can drive include school buses, passenger buses, tankers and doubles and triples.

6. The correct answer is: (C). A Commercial Learner's Permit.

CLP means Commercial Learner's Permit. This permit is usually issued to applicants between 18 and 20 and below the 21-year age requirement for the Commercial Driver's License. With this permit, a driver can operate commercial vehicles within the state until he/she is 21 years old.

7. The correct answer is: (C). CDL drivers cannot take illegal drugs and also some legal drugs are prohibited.

The DOT Testing panel screens drivers for drug use, and in the list are both legal and illegal drugs that are prohibited.

8. The correct answer is: (D). All of the above.

Even though some drugs are legal and may have a prescription, if they are found to slow down reaction time and are deemed to affect the driver to a point of high risk, a driver may be disqualified.

9. The correct answer is: (B). Every 2 years.

DOT Physical tests include drug tests administered by a physician. The test can take anywhere from 30 minutes to an hour to complete.

10. The correct answer is: (C). The Commercial Motor Vehicle Safety Act.

On October 27, 1986, the US government enacted the Commercial Motor Vehicle Safety Act to enforce the licensing requirement and outline the penalty for violations.

11. The correct answer is: (C). Three classes.

A Commercial Driver's License is classified into three classes. These are Class A, Class B, and Class C. Each driver's license class permits the holder to operate the vehicles covered by the class. Hence, if you hold a Class A license, you can't operate vehicles covered by Class B.

12. The correct answer is: (D). Two or more vehicles with a combined weight of over 26,000 pounds.

The Class A license allows its holder to drive two or more vehicles. The combined weight of the two vehicles should exceed 26,000 pounds.

13. The correct answer is: (C). SUVs.

As a Class A driver's license holder, you can operate a wide range of commercial vehicles. These include tractor-trailers, flatbeds, tanks, school bus and passenger buses with a specific number of passengers. This license class doesn't cover small vehicles, family cars and SUVs.

14. The correct answer is: (C). 16 passengers.

The P Endorsement allows holders to drive a passenger vehicle that can transport a minimum of 16 passengers. You must pass the Passenger Transport Road Skills Test and the Passenger Transport Knowledge Test in order to receive the endorsement.

15. The correct answer is: (C). The Transportation Safety Administration.

TSA is the acronym for the Transportation Safety Administration. The administration is responsible for the safety of the roads, drivers and pedestrians, among others.

16. The correct answer is: (A). Tanks.

There are different types of endorsements. They include the N Endorsement, P Endorsement and a host of others, all allowing holders to operate various vehicles.

17. The correct answer is: (C). S Endorsement.

The S Endorsement is for individuals who want to drive school buses. Before you get the endorsement, you must pass the relevant tests.

18. The correct answer is: (D). New Hampshire.

Nearly all states allow drivers to operate double or triple trailers provided they have the required endorsement. However, New Hampshire is the lone state that doesn't allow the operation of triple vehicles.

19. The correct answer is: (B). Class B.

The Class B license is issued to drivers who operate commercial vehicles with a combination weight of over 26,000 pounds. Licensed drivers can drive box trucks, straight trucks, tractor-trailers and segmented buses.

20. The correct answer is: (D). Class C.

If you have the appropriate endorsement on your Class B driver's license, you can drive vehicles that are usually for Class C license holders. This is because endorsements offer the holders some exceptions that allow them to operate vehicles under other license classes. Check the available endorsement for your license.

21. The correct answer is: (B). Class B.

You can drive trucks, segmented buses, large buses and straight trucks with the Class B license. Other vehicles you can operate with this class of license include delivery trucks, tow trucks and garbage trucks. You can also tow a vehicle that weighs less than 10,000 pounds.

22. The correct answer is: (A). Class C.

If you wish to transport hazardous materials, you can apply for the Class C license. With the license, you can transport flammable liquids, a wide range of gases, combustible liquids and explosives. You can also transport propane, gasoline, chlorine, hydrochloric acid, ammonia and sulfuric acid.

23. The correct answer is: (A). Medium truck and weighs between 10,000 pounds and 14,000 pounds.

Class 3 trucks are not too heavy and not too light either.

24. The correct answer is: (A). Heavy truck and weighs more than 33,000 pounds.

Class 8 Trucks are the heaviest from the category of trucks.

25. The correct answer is: (B). 80%.

A driver is deemed qualified to receive the Commercial Driver's License if he/she scores a minimum of 80% on the exam. Anything short of that is considered an automatic disqualification from obtaining the license. This underscores the importance of thoroughly preparing for the test.

26. The correct answer is: (B). A Medium truck and weighs between 14,000 pounds and 16,000 pounds.

There are multiple classes of medium trucks and Class 4 is one of them.

27. The correct answer is: (C). Heavy truck and weighs between 26,000 pounds and 33,000 pounds.

A Class 7 Truck is a heavy truck just like a Class 8 truck. There are only two classes of heavy trucks: Class 7 and Class 8.

28. The correct answer is: (A). Medium truck and weighs between 16,000 pounds and 19,500 pounds.

Class 5 trucks are medium trucks, and in total there are 4 classes of medium trucks.

29. The correct answer is: (A). Credit history.

There is a long list of documents that you can present as proof of identity. This includes a government-issued identity card, your birth certificate and U. S. military discharge papers. Your credit history is not considered proof of identity.

30. The correct answer is: (D). Duplicate documents and original copies of your documents.

Photocopies of your documents are not acceptable. Duplicates and original documents are acceptable.

31. The correct answer is: (A). Certificate of citizenship and birth certificate.

You need your birth certificate and certificate of citizenship to prove your permanent residency or citizenship. You can't prove your citizenship or residency with other documents such as a work permit or utility bills. Contact your local DMV for a list of acceptable documents.

32. The correct answer is: (A). IRS W-2 form.

The IRS W-2 form contains a list of other documents you can use to prove your residency. The form is otherwise known as an income tax return.

33. The correct answer is: (C). The DMV must decide.

When filling out the Commercial Driver's License application online, make sure that your name matches the one on your ID or any other document you intend to use as proof of identity. If the names don't match, you may be disqualified from taking the test.

34. The correct answer is: (B). Two weeks.

If you hold a Commercial Learner's Permit and wish to apply for the Commercial Driver's License, you must wait for 14 days.

35. The correct answer is: (B). 21 years.

In most states, you must be at least 21 years old before you are considered eligible for a driver's license. Such states may issue you a learner's permit if you are between 18 and 20 years old. However, your driving will be restricted to your state of residence.

36. The correct answer is: (C). 18 and 20

Applicants between ages 18 and 20 are restricted to intrastate transports until they are 21. At that age, their learner's permit will be replaced with a driver's license to enable them to operate across the country.

37. The correct answer is: (C). 21 years.

If you hold a Commercial Learner's Permit that restricts your activities to your state of residence, it expires once you are 21 years old. At the age, you have become an adult and can drive commercial vehicles across the country with your driver's license.

38. The correct answer is: (C). 21 years.

The minimum age for interstate driving is 21. Before 21, you won't be allowed to drive outside your state with your learner's permit.

39. The correct answer is: (D). None of the above.

The examination body can disqualify applicants based on several factors. If you can't produce proof of identity on request, your application will be disqualified. The same applies if you can't speak or write English fluently or if you present an expired ID.

40. The correct answer is: (C). The driver can't overturn the decision.

If you have been disqualified from driving in the past for any serious offense, you are automatically banned for life. You can't overturn the decision, meaning that you will never be allowed to get behind a wheel again.

41. The correct answer is: (A). 20/40.

Commercial drivers must have 20/40 vision in each eye. This is to prevent vision-related accidents.

42. The correct answer is: (B). 140 degrees or higher.

For horizontal vision, a driver is expected to have 140 degrees or higher. The goal is to ensure that such a driver won't have issues with seeing horizontal objects.

43. The correct answer is: (D). All of the above.

You may be disqualified from taking the exam if you are found with electronic devices such as cell phones or notes. Entering the test center with personal effects is also an invitation to disqualification.

44. The correct answer is: (A). A year-long ban from applying for the license.

A year-long ban awaits drivers that are guilty of driving under the influence of drugs or alcohol. This is to serve as a deterrent to other drivers who may be considering driving under the influence. It also ensures the security of drivers, passengers, pedestrians and other motorists.

45. The correct answer is: (C). Below 0.04.

The acceptable blood alcohol content for drivers of commercial motor vehicles is below 0.04. A blood alcohol content that exceeds this limit may result in stiff penalties.

46. The correct answer is: (D). 60 days to life ban.

The offender may be banned from driving for 60 days. However, depending on various factors, he/she may also face a lifetime driving ban.

47. The correct answer is: (D). You will be banned for a year.

The government penalizes drivers who use their vehicles for illegal or criminal activities. Such a crime is a felony. If you are found guilty of committing this crime with a commercial vehicle, you stand the risk of being banned from driving a commercial vehicle for a year.

48. The correct answer is: (A). A lifetime ban.

If you are convicted of manufacturing or distributing drugs illegally with a commercial motor vehicle, the penalty is a lifetime driving ban.

49. The correct answer is: (D). A year-long ban.

If you are involved in an accident that leads to a loss of life or injury, you must stop at the scene of the accident. Fleeing the scene may result in a one-year driving ban.

50. The correct answer is: (A) Double or triple trailers.

The endorsement allows you to drive either a double or triple trailer. As an applicant for the T endorsement, you must pass the Doubles/Triples Knowledge Test.

Air Brakes Test 1 – 25 Questions

1. Air brakes are otherwise known as a ...
    a. Compressed air brake system.
    b. Compressed air braking system.
    c. Compressed pressure air brake system.
    d. Compressed pressure air braking system.

2. The brake system is powered by ...
    a. Compressed air.
    b. Pressurized air.
    c. All of the above.
    d. None of the above.

3. The part of the brake system that is responsible for stopping the vehicle is the ...
    a. Brake pad.
    b. Brake pressure.
    c. Brake shoe.
    d. Brake stopper.

4. The primary difference between vehicles with air brakes and those with hydraulic fluid is that ...
    a. Air brakes are not affected by leaks while hydraulic brakes are.
    b. Hydraulic brakes are not affected by leaks while air brakes are.
    c. There is no significant difference between the two.
    d. Air brakes are more expensive than hydraulic brakes.

5. Reliability is one of the major factors behind the rising popularity of ...
    a. Hydraulic fluid-based brake systems.
    b. Air brake systems.
    c. Both brake systems.
    d. Neither brake system.

6. ... developed air brakes for use in railways.
    a. George Washington.
    b. George Barbados.
    c. George Westinghouse.
    d. George Stones.

7. Which of the following need to be checked when doing air brake inspection?
    a. Slack adjusters, drums, linings.
    b. Slack adjusters, drums, linings, hoses.
    c. Slack adjusters, drums, hoses.
    d. Slac adjusters, linings, hoses.

8. ... are the most common air brake systems.
    a. Common brakes.
    b. Foundation brakes.
    c. Superb brakes.
    d. Permanent brakes.

9. The components that hold enough air for brakes to use repeatedly are the ...
    a. Air containers.
    b. Air reservoir tanks.
    c. Air storage tanks.
    d. Air preservation tanks.

10. This component pumps air into the reservoir tank.
    a. Air pump.
    b. Air release mechanism.
    c. Air compressor.
    d. Air distributor.

11. What function does the slack adjuster perform?
    a. It connects the push rod and the brake through its arm.
    b. It connects the push rod and the brake chambers.
    c. It connects the air compressor and the push rod.
    d. It connects the brake chambers and the brake.

12. The brake pedal is otherwise known as ...
    a. The foot valve.
    b. The brake engager.
    c. The brake depressor.
    d. The brake applier.

13. The ... reduces the risk of the air brake valves freezing up.
    a. Air evaporator.
    b. Alcohol evaporator.
    c. Ice breaker.
    d. None of the above.

14. Two major contaminants of air tank drains are ... and ...
    a. Water and oil.
    b. Water and dirt.
    c. Oil and other particles.
    d. All of the above.

15. This type of air tank comes equipped with electric heating devices.
    a. Electrical air tanks.
    b. Manual air tanks.
    c. Automatic air tanks.
    d. Hybrid air tanks.

16. Spring brakes serve what purpose in the air brake?
    a. They provide the mechanical force that prevents accidental leakage of air pressure.
    b. They are used for holding the brake pedals together.
    c. They establish a connection between the alcohol evaporator and the return spring.
    d. They protect the brake from excessive pressure.

17. Air brakes are fully operational when the air pressure drops to ...
    a. Between 30 and 40 psi.
    b. Between 15 and 20 psi.
    c. Between 20 and 30 psi.
    d. Between 30 and 50 psi.

18. What should you do when the buzzer and low air pressure warning light flashes?
    a. Stop the vehicle while you can still control the brake.
    b. Drive for as long as possible.
    c. Drive until you can stop the warning signals.
    d. Do nothing.

19. Braking power is dependent on ...
    a. How the brakes are adjusted.
    b. The air pressure in the brake system.
    c. The parking brake controls.
    d. The types of drain valves in the brake system.

20. Which valve doesn't need assistance to expel water and oil?
    a. Manual valve.
    b. Hybrid valve.
    c. Automatic valve.
    d. All of the above.

21. The major cause of brake failure in cold weather is ...
    a. Bad roads.
    b. The water in the tank may freeze.
    c. The brake pedals cracking due to cold water.
    d. The alcohol to prevent freezing was not circulated properly in the system.

22. Which part of the air brake separates the brakes and pushes them against the brake drum?
    a. The brake S-Cam.
    b. The safety valve.
    c. The air compressor governor.
    d. The slack adjuster.

23. A steel rod in the air brake that shares some similarities with the piston connecting the brake chamber and the slack adjuster is ...
    a. The brake rod.
    b. The connecting rod.
    c. The push rod.
    d. The slacking rod.

24. A lined steel mechanism that produces friction when it comes in contact with the brake drum is the ...
    a. Brake lining.
    b. Brake compartment.
    c. Brake shoe.
    d. Brake connector.

25. Why is it important to drain the air tank regularly?
    a. It prevents brake malfunctioning by preventing contaminants from affecting the brakes.
    b. It provides room for more air in the air tank.
    c. It is a preventive measure against corrosion.
    d. It purifies the stored air.

Air Brakes Test 1 Answers

1. The correct answer is: (A). Compressed air brake system.

Another name for air brakes is a compressed air brake system. This is classified as a friction brake and is commonly found in vehicles that use compressed air for braking.

2. The correct answer is: (A). Compressed air.

While some brake systems are powered by hydraulic fluid, the air brake system is powered by compressed air. The compressed air presses on the piston and applies the brake to the brake pad.

3. The correct answer is: (A). A brake pad.

The brake pad is the part of the brake system responsible for stopping the vehicle. When pressure is applied on the brake pad, it exerts pressure on the brakes and the brakes are applied. When there is no pressure on the brake pad, the brakes are released.

4. The correct answer is: (A). Air brakes are not affected by leaks while hydraulic brakes are.

The primary difference between vehicles that use brakes powered by hydraulic fluid and those with brakes powered by air is that while hydraulic fluids may leak and lead to brake failure, air brakes are not affected by leaks. Hence, brake failure is limited to the barest minimum.

5. The correct answer is: (B). The air brake system.

The air brake system is noted for its reliability. Drivers can rest assured that they won't run out of fluid to power their brakes. This makes this type of brake more reliable than others.

6. The correct answer is: (C). George Westinghouse.

Air brakes were initially developed for use in railways by George Westinghouse. Thanks to their reliability, air brakes gradually became an integral part of modern commercial motor vehicles.

7. The correct answer is: (B). Slack adjusters, drums, linings, hoses.

All of these parts need to be inspected during the air brake inspection.

8. The correct answer is: (B). Foundation brakes.

Air brakes are otherwise known as foundation brakes. They are found in buses and trucks. This braking system adopts the triple-valve principle that is common in rail cars. It can cause the exhaustion of the brake cylinder and thus release the brakes in the process.

9. The correct answer is: (B). Air reservoir tanks.

The air reservoir tanks are the components of the air brakes that hold enough air for the brakes to use repeatedly. As long as there is air in the air reservoir tanks, the brakes will function correctly.

10. The correct answer is: (C). The air compressor.

The air compressor is the air brake component that pumps the air the brake needs for operation into the air reservoir tank.

11. The correct answer is: (A). It connects the push rod and the brake through its arm.

The slack adjuster plays a crucial role in the operation of the air brakes. It connects the push rod and the brake through its arm. This makes it possible to control the distance between the two brake shoes. With the reduced distance between them, braking is easier and faster.

12. The correct answer is: (A). The foot valve.

Another name for the brake pedal is foot valve. It releases air from the reservoir tanks. When you remove the pressure by lifting your foot, the brake is disengaged and the air pressure is reduced. When you release the brakes, the system releases some air.

13. The correct answer is: (B). Alcohol evaporator.

An alcohol evaporator is the air brake system component that is used for putting alcohol into the system. This comes in handy in colder climates. It reduces the risk of the air brake valves freezing over.

14. The correct answer is: (A). Water and oil.

Water and oil are two major contaminants common in air tank drains. They may settle at the bottom of the tank and cause a malfunction in the braking system. Thus, it is imperative that you drain the air tank regularly.

15. The correct answer is: (B). Manual air tanks.

A challenge that is common to air tanks during cold weather is the freezing of water in the tanks. This can lead to brake failure. Manual air tanks come fully equipped with electric heating devices to prevent freezing.

16. The correct answer is: (A). They provide the mechanical force that prevents accidental leakage of air pressure.

Truck tractors, trucks and buses are all equipped with parking and emergency brakes. They are held together by mechanical force to prevent accidental leakage of the air pressure. Spring brakes provide the air brake with the mechanical force it needs to prevent accidental leakage of the air pressure.

17. The correct answer is: (C). Between 20 and 30 psi.

Straight trucks and tractor have spring brakes too. The brakes are fully operational when the air pressure in the brake drops to between 20 and 30 psi. At that stage, it may not be advisable to wait until the brakes are automatically applied.

18. The correct answer is: (A). Stop the vehicle while you can still control the brake.

As soon as the buzzer and low air pressure warning light flash, you should stop the vehicle. Waiting until a more convenient time could lead to an accident.

19. The correct answer is: (A). How the brakes are adjusted.

The braking power is dependent on how the brakes are adjusted. In badly adjusted brakes, the regular brakes won't work. The parking/emergency brakes will malfunction as well.

20. The correct answer is: (C). Automatic valve.

There are two types of drain valves. One is operated manually by pulling a cable or turning a quarter turn. After completing your activities for the day, drain the tanks. The automatic valve expels oil and water automatically.

21. The correct answer is: (B). The water in the tank may freeze.

The major cause of brake failure in cold weather is water freezing in the air tank. This problem has been corrected with the introduction of automatic air tanks equipped with electric heating devices.

22. The correct answer is: (A). Brake S-Cam.

The brake, shaped in the form of the letter "S," separates the brakes by pushing them apart and pushing them against the brake drum. Approximately 85% of vehicles that use air brakes in the US are equipped with the S-Cam.

23. The correct answer is: (C). The push rod.

The push rod is a steel rod in the air brake that shares some similarities with the piston connecting the brake chamber and the slack adjuster. When the rod is depressed, the brakes are immediately released. Extending the push rod automatically applies the brakes.

24. The correct answer is: (C). The brake shoe.

The brake shoe is a lined steel mechanism that produces friction when it comes in contact with the brake drum. It uses friction to stop a moving vehicle when the brakes are applied. Thus, it is crucial to the efficiency of the braking system.

25. The correct answer is: (A). It prevents brake malfunctioning by preventing contaminants from affecting the brakes.

Brake failure can be caused by two factors. Contaminants such as water and oil may affect the efficiency of the braking system when they settle at the bottom of the air tank. By draining the air tank regularly, such contaminants can't settle.

Hazmat Test 1 – 25 Questions

1. Hazmat means ...
   a. Hazardous matters.
   b. Hazardous materials.
   c. Hazardous metallic substances.
   d. None of the above.

2. Flammable solids such as ... are typical examples of hazmat.
   a. Matches and fuses.
   b. Gasoline and ammonia.
   c. Acetone and chlorine.
   d. Fuses and sulfuric acid.

3. Two major factors that determine the hazardous nature of a substance are ...
   a. Characteristics and shipper's decision.
   b. Shipper's decision and shipping technique.
   c. Characteristics and nature.
   d. Weight and characteristics.

4. The hazmat test should be taken in ...
   a. French and English.
   b. English.
   c. French.
   d. In a driver's preferred language.

5. Which of the following shows that a material is hazardous?
   a. It's placarded with an X or RQ.
   b. A diamond label.
   c. All of the above.
   d. None of the above.

6. The following usually are classified as hazardous materials:
   a. Fireworks and pest control.
   b. Chemical supplies and pencils.
   c. Agricultural materials and books.
   d. Paints.

7. These endorsements are associated with transporting hazmat.
    a. H or X.
    b. G or P.
    c. K or L.
    d. D and H.

8. To qualify for a Commercial Driver's License to transport hazardous materials, you must:
    a. Take a security threat assessment test and be aged 21 and above.
    b. Take part in a security threat assessment test and be aged 18 and above.
    c. Take part in a security threat assessment test and be between 18 and 21.
    d. Take part in a security threat assessment test and be above 30 years old.

9. For your CDL renewal, you are expected to provide up to a ... history of the licenses you have held in the past.
    a. 15-year.
    b. 8-year.
    c. 10-year.
    d. 18-year.

10. To qualify for the CDL Hazmat license, you must pass the ...
    a. TSA Hazmat Security Assessment.
    b. BSA Security Threat Assessment.
    c. TSA Security Threat Assessment.
    d. BSA Hazmat Security Threat Assessment.

11. The TSA test rule was established on ...
    a. May 10, 1890.
    b. May 5, 1980.
    c. May 5, 2003.
    d. May 10, 2008.

12. You have ... to complete the TSA assessment after submitting your fingerprints.
    a. 20 days.
    b. 15 days.
    c. 30 days.
    d. 45 days.

13. The assessment completion date can be extended if ...
    a. You have eligibility issues.
    b. You apply for an extension.
    c. There are insufficient materials for the test.
    d. The examiner deems it fit to extend the date.

14. You can be permanently barred from getting the hazardous materials endorsement if ...
    a. You are late to the exam center.
    b. You fail to complete the test.
    c. You fail the test three times in a row.
    d. You have a criminal record.

15. Which of these crimes incur automatic disqualification from the hazmat endorsement?
    a. Espionage and sedition.
    b. Treason and theft.
    c. Public fighting and excessive speeding.
    d. All of the above.

16. You are forbidden from taking this test if you are ...
    a. A fugitive.
    b. A feminist.
    c. An animal rights activist.
    d. A social activist.

17. Other crimes that may prevent you from taking the test include all of the following except:
    a. Arson and kidnapping.
    b. Environmental damage and disruption of the transportation system.
    c. Tax evasion and hostage taking.
    d. None of the above.

18. You can challenge a ban if you have proof of the following:
    a. US citizenship or permanent residency.
    b. Mistaken identity and reversed conviction.
    c. International driver's license and international passport.
    d. Years of experience in the military or public health sector.

19. You have the right to apply for a waiver if you have proof of:
    a. Acknowledgment of conviction based on reason of insanity.
    b. Acknowledgement of conviction based on a strong personal conviction.
    c. Accidental murder or manslaughter.
    d. A and C.

20. The TSA will respond to your waiver application within ...
    a. 10 days of the receipt of your waiver application.
    b. 5 days of the receipt of your waiver application.
    c. 15 days of the receipt of your waiver application.
    d. 30 days of the receipt of your waiver application.

21. Which of these crimes doesn't mean disqualification?
    a. Roadside infractions.
    b. Placarding violations.
    c. Bribery.
    d. A and B.

22. The Security Threat Assessment is conducted by the ...
    a. Transportation Security Arbitrators.
    b. Transportation Security Amendment Body.
    c. Transportation Security Association.
    d. Transportation Security Administration.

23. Which of the following criteria must you meet to be eligible for the hazmat endorsement?
    a. State government criteria only.
    b. Federal government criteria only.
    c. State and federal government criteria.
    d. State criteria is mandatory while federal criteria is optional.

24. When inspecting the tanks used for transporting hazardous materials, check for the following:
    a. Diamond labels on the premises.
    b. Placard labels on the premises.
    c. None of the listed signs.
    d. All of the listed signs.

25. The safest transportation vessel for hazardous materials is ...
    a. Any type of commercial vehicle.
    b. Planes and ships.
    c. Heavy commercial vehicles.
    d. All of the above.

Hazmat Test 1 Answers

1. The correct answer is: (B). Hazmat means hazardous materials.

Hazmat means hazardous materials. This is in reference to substances that are injurious to health and can damage property and/or be a serious threat to public health.

2. The correct answer is: (A). Matches and fuses.

Matches and fuses are some typical examples of flammable solids that can constitute serious health hazards. The list of hazardous materials includes flammable liquids, a wide range of gas, combustible liquids, explosives, propane, gasoline, chlorine, hydrochloric acid and ammonia.

3. The correct answer is: (A). Characteristics and shipper's decision.

Characteristics and a shipper's decision are two major factors that determine whether a substance is hazardous or not. When shipping such materials, the shipper makes transporters aware of the nature of a substance by indicating whether it is hazardous or not.

4. The correct answer is: (B). English only.

The hazmat test is conducted in English only. Thus, a driver must understand, read and speak English before being eligible to take the test.

5. The correct answer is: (C). All of the above.

One of the ways you can identify a hazardous substance is by its label(s). A substance with an RQ or X label in the right column is hazardous. The shipper will also use placards or diamond labels to notify people of a substance's hazardous nature.

6. The correct answer is: (A). Fireworks and pest control.

Pest control chemicals and fireworks usually release hazardous materials. Hence, if you are hired to help with the distribution of these products, you will need an endorsement for transporting hazardous materials.

7. The correct answer is: (A). An H or X endorsement.

With either of these endorsements on your CDL, you can legally transport hazardous materials.

8. The correct answer is: (A). You must take part in a security threat assessment and be aged 21 and above.

You must meet some requirements to qualify for an endorsement to transport hazardous materials in the United States. Some of these requirements include passing a security threat assessment conducted by the TSA as well as being at least 21 years old.

9. The correct answer is: (C). 10 years.

For your CDL renewal, you are required to provide a history of your previous licenses. If possible, you must provide licenses that cover the past 10 years if you are not new in the trucking industry. This is irrespective of your state of residence or type of license.

10. The correct answer is: (C). A TSA Security Threat Assessment.

To qualify for the type of CDL that permits you to transport hazardous materials, it is mandatory that you pass the TSA Security Threat Assessment.

11. The correct answer is: (C). May 5, 2003.

The TSA test rule was made public on May 5, 2003, when the TSA published the 49 CFR 1572 rule under which the TSA is required to conduct the threat assessment. The goal is to ensure that hazardous substances are properly and safely transported across the country.

12. The correct answer is: (C). 30 days.

You are expected to complete the assessment within 30 days of submitting your fingerprints to the examiner. Failure to do this will result in your application being disqualified. However, the submission deadline may be extended depending on certain circumstances.

13. The correct answer is: (A). You have eligibility issues.

The assessment completion can be extended under two conditions. These are if you have eligibility issues or your paperwork is incomplete. In either case, the extension is to allow you or the TSA to fix the issues without delay so you can take the exam.

14. The correct answer is: (D). You have a criminal record.

You will be permanently barred from getting the hazardous materials endorsement if you have a criminal record. These include a record of terrorism-related crimes and others that include rape, money laundering and kidnapping.

15. The correct answer is: (A). Espionage and sedition.

Sedition and espionage rank very high among the crimes that may incur an automatic disqualification from getting a hazmat endorsement on your driver's license. These and other related crimes are considered serious enough to undermine the country's security and thus the examiner won't give such individuals access to harmful substances.

16. The correct answer is: (A). A fugitive.

As a fugitive, you can't take the test. The same rule applies to non-US citizens, individuals who are not permanent residents, those who have been medically certified as not mentally competent to handle commercial vehicles or who have involuntarily received medical attention at a mental institution.

17. The correct answer is: (D). None of the above.

Any applicant who has committed any of the crimes listed here can't take the test. This includes kidnappers, arsonists and hostage takers. Others who are not allowed to take the test are applicants with a tax evasion history and individuals who are guilty of damaging the environment or disrupting the transportation system.

18. The correct answer is: (B). Mistaken identity and reversed conviction.

You can challenge a ban if you can prove a case of mistaken identity when you were accused of a crime that got you disqualified from taking the test. You should also be able to prove that a conviction was reversed.

19. The correct answer is: (A). Acknowledgment of conviction based on reason of insanity.

Some extenuating circumstances allow you to apply for a waiver if you are disqualified. These are acknowledgment of conviction based on reason of insanity or acknowledgement of being involuntarily committed to a mental institution.

20. The correct answer is: (D). 30 days of the receipt of your waiver application.

Once you submit a waiver request, the TSA will respond within 30 days of the receipt of your application. In the meantime, you can hone your skills and keep preparing for the test.

21. The correct answer is: (D). Both A and B. Roadside infractions and placarding violations.

Although you may be disqualified on multiple grounds, you can't be disqualified for placarding violations or roadside infractions.

22. The correct answer is: (D). The Transportation Security Administration.

The Security Threat Assessment is conducted by the Transportation Security Administration. This body is responsible for regulating the activities of the transportation industry with a view to ensuring safer roads by providing guidelines and enforcing training. As drivers are trained to be more security conscious, the roads become safer.

23. The correct answer is: (C). State and federal governments.

To be eligible for any type of endorsement, including one that allows you to transport hazardous materials, you must meet both state and federal government criteria.

24. The correct answer is: (D). All of the listed signs.

To determine whether a tank is used for transporting hazardous materials or not, check the placard and diamond labels.

25. The correct answer is: (C). In heavy commercial vehicles.

Although there are several options when considering how to transport hazardous materials, the best and safest way to transport them is in heavy commercial vehicles.

Combination Vehicles Test 1 – 25 Questions

1. If you can handle a wide range of heavy commercial vehicles, you must pass the ...
    a. Heavy vehicles test.
    b. Combination vehicle test.
    c. Heavy commercial vehicles test.
    d. All of the above.

2. Some attributes of combination vehicles that differentiate them from other commercial vehicles include ...
    a. They are heavier and longer.
    b. They are more expensive and longer.
    c. They require different licenses to drive.
    d. They break down easily.

3. Combination vehicle drivers must ...
    a. Have excellent knowledge of the roads and their vehicle.
    b. Have excellent driving experience and top-notch knowledge of their vehicle.
    c. Be more experienced than drivers of other vehicles.
    d. Have five years of driving experience.

4. Which test comes first?
    a. The driving test.
    b. The written test.
    c. The knowledge test.
    d. The ability test.

5. A combination of vehicles is otherwise known as ...
    a. A semitruck.
    b. A semitrailer.
    c. A semitruck-trailer.
    d. A semi-tanker.

6. Combination vehicles can easily bend in the middle thanks to a ...
    a. Fifth-wheel dolly.
    b. Fifth-wheel converter.
    c. Fifth-wheel bender.
    d. Fifth-wheel combination connector.

7. Which of the following is easier to stop?
    a. An empty truck.
    b. A fully loaded truck.
    c. A half-full truck.
    d. A new truck.

8. What is jackknifing?
    a. A condition in which a fully-loaded combination vehicle stops abruptly.
    b. A condition in which the vehicle bends into a V shape while skidding uncontrollably.
    c. The joining of vehicles with a converter dolly.
    d. Easily stopping an empty truck.

9. ... is the primary cause of jackknifing.
    a. Loss of traction.
    b. Loss of direction.
    c. Speeding.
    d. Careless braking at corners.

10. Jackknifing is common to what types of combination vehicles?
    a. Empty trailers.
    b. Fully loaded trailers.
    c. Trailers with badly distributed loads.
    d. Both A and B.

11. What must you avoid when driving on a curve?
    a. Decelerating and braking sharply.
    b. Looking at the vehicles behind.
    c. Honking your horn.
    d. All of the above.

12. One way to guard against jackknifing is to ...
    a. Spread your braking over a distance.
    b. Break at intervals.
    c. Apply the brakes at your convenience.
    d. Honk the horn before applying the brakes.

13. A prelude to jackknifing is ...
    a. Skidding.
    b. Braking.
    c. Horn honking.
    d. Overtaking.

14. You can avoid a wide range of braking-related problems if ...
    a. You apply the brakes regularly.
    b. You drive with full concentration on your brakes.
    c. You pay attention to your environment.
    d. You don't panic when you apply the brakes suddenly.

15. What is cheating?
    a. A situation in which both the rear and front wheels take different paths.
    b. When the brakes fail to function properly after applying them.
    c. When you are forced to give way to a reckless driver who overtakes you carelessly.
    d. A situation that tests your driving skills when negotiating a bend.

16. You can control cheating by ...
    a. Ensuring no vehicle overtakes you carelessly.
    b. Ensuring that your brakes are in good condition.
    c. Focusing on the front wheels.
    d. None of the above.

17. A preventive measure against getting stuck on railroad tracks is ...
    a. Not shifting gears while crossing railroad tracks.
    b. Shifting gears midway while crossing railroad tracks.
    c. Stopping your vehicle when necessary on the railroad tracks.
    d. Paying attention to your environment while crossing railroad tracks.

18. What role does a DOT placard play while crossing a public railroad?
    a. It contains a number you can call for immediate assistance during emergencies.
    b. It contains driving information such as the speed limit.
    c. It contains information about the nearest gas station.
    d. It provides weather information.

19. Backing up a combination vehicle is otherwise known as ...
    a. Reversing.
    b. Automatic braking.
    c. Speeding up.
    d. Careful driving.

20. Poor backing is responsible for ... of road accidents involving combination vehicles.
    a. 20%.
    b. 40%.
    c. 35%.
    d. 25%.

21. The most common areas where backing-related accidents occur are ...
    a. Residential driveways and highways.
    b. Highways and parking lots.
    c. Parking lots and residential highways.
    d. Residential driveways and parking lots.

22. What is the GOAL approach?
    a. A definite place to back up your vehicle.
    b. Inspecting your environment while backing up.
    c. An approach that highlights the importance of using seat belts.
    d. Paying attention to potential dangers during driving.

23. Who is a spotter?
    a. Someone who spots law enforcement agencies in advance.
    b. Someone who checks your environment for potential obstacles while backing up.
    c. Someone who helps with identifying problems in a combination vehicle.
    d. Someone who helps you identify the best place to park your vehicle.

24. It is advisable to tap your horn ... while reversing.
    a. Twice.
    b. Four times.
    c. Eight times.
    d. As many times as necessary.

25. To prevent reversing-related accidents and problems, install a ... in your vehicle.
    a. Distance alarm.
    b. Rear-vision camera.
    c. Contact sensor.
    d. All of the above.

Combination Vehicle Test 1 Answers

1. The correct answer is: (B). A combination vehicle test.

If you can handle a wide range of heavy commercial vehicles, you must pass the combination vehicle test. This test is specifically designed for commercial vehicle drivers who specialize in operating combination vehicles of any type.

2. The correct answer is: (A). They are heavier and longer.

Some attributes of combination vehicles such as longer size and heavier weight distinguish them from other vehicles in the combination class. Their sheer length and weight requires drivers to have some special driving skills before they can operate such vehicles without issues.

3. The correct answer is: (B). Have excellent driving experience and top-notch knowledge of the vehicle.

Even if you have operated other types of commercial vehicles, combination vehicles are a different ball game. You need special driving experience before you sit behind the wheel.

4. The correct answer is: (B). A written test.

While both the written and driving tests are very important, each applicant is expected to take the written test first. It is a test of your theoretical knowledge of combination vehicles before you attempt the practical test.

5. The correct answer is: (A). Semitruck.

A combination of vehicles is otherwise known as a semitruck or semi. It is a combination of a tractor unit and a trailer or many trailers. The connection between the tractor and the trailer(s) is made with a converter dolly or fifth-wheel dolly. Sometimes, both dollies can be used.

6. The correct answer is: (A). A fifth-wheel dolly.

Combination vehicles can easily bend in the middle because of the fifth-wheel dolly used for connecting the tractor unit and the attached trailer or trailers.

7. The correct answer is: (B). A fully-loaded truck.

While combination vehicles are more difficult to stop than a regular car, a fully loaded truck is still easier to stop than an empty truck. Thus, when handling an empty truck, you must be extremely careful when you brake.

8. The correct answer is: (B). It is a condition in which the vehicle bends into a V shape while skidding uncontrollably.

Jackknifing is a common problem to combination vehicles, thanks to their length. It is a condition in which a combination vehicle bends into a V or L shape. This is more common when the vehicle skids uncontrollably and may cause problems including rollovers.

9. The correct answer is: (A). A loss of traction.

Loss of traction is the primary cause of jackknifing. Loss of traction occurs when there is low friction between the tires and the road. This may be caused by gravel, sand, ice, snow or any other substance that causes tires to lose their grip on the road surface.

10. The correct answer is: (D). Both A and B. Empty trailers and fully-loaded trailers.

Jackknifing is common to empty trailers and trailers with badly distributed loads. This is because stopping an empty vehicle is usually more difficult than stopping a fully loaded one. More so, uneven distribution of the loads carried by a combination vehicle may make it unbalanced, causing jackknifing.

11. The correct answer is: (A). Decelerating and braking sharply.

A preventive measure against accidents when driving on a curve is to avoid braking and decelerating sharply. Either of the two actions may result in a rollover or a more serious accident.

12. The correct answer is: (A). Spread your braking over a distance.

An effective preventive measure against jackknifing is spreading your braking over a reasonable distance. If you don't brake suddenly, the vehicle won't jackknife.

13. The correct answer is: (A).Skidding.

Jackknifing doesn't occur suddenly. When you apply the brakes suddenly, the vehicle may skid. Skidding will then trigger jackknifing. Thus, any driving-related problem that can cause skidding will also increase a vehicle's tendency to jackknife. Watch out for such problems and avoid them.

14. The correct answer is: (C). Pay attention to your environment.

Most braking-related problems are avoidable if you take the necessary precautions. This includes paying attention to your environment, identifying potential problems and avoiding them. This includes blind spots and potholes.

15. The correct answer is: (A). A situation in which both the rear and front wheels take different paths.

In combination vehicles, cheating is a common problem that may lead to skidding, and by extension, jackknifing. It is a situation that arises when both the rear and front wheels take different paths. The rear wheels won't take the same path as the front wheels.

16. The correct answer is: (C). Focusing on the front wheels.

Cheating can be controlled and corrected. To prevent skidding or jackknifing, focus on the front wheels. If properly controlled, the rear wheels won't go out of control, even if they follow a different path.

17. The correct answer is: (A). Not shifting gears while crossing railroad tracks.

You may get stuck on railroad tracks when driving a combination vehicle if you don't take necessary precautions. To avoid this, under no condition should you shift gears while crossing railroad tracks. Do that either before or after crossing the tracks.

18. The correct answer is: (A). It contains a number you can call for immediate assistance.

If you are stuck on the tracks, you can call for immediate assistance by locating the number on the DOT sign.

19. The correct answer is: (A). Reversing.

Backing up is also known as reversing. Backing up a combination vehicle is very risky and should be done with extreme caution. It is not advisable to back up on a highway with such a long and heavy vehicle. You should only reverse the vehicle when absolutely necessary.

20. The correct answer is: (D). 25%.

The National Safety Council reports that approximately 25% of vehicle accidents can be attributed to poor reversing. Over 500 deaths and 15,000 injuries are caused by reversing-related accidents. Hence, be cautious when backing up a combination vehicle.

21. The correct answer is: (D). Residential driveways and parking lots.

The US National Highway Traffic Safety Administration reports that most backing-up-related accidents occur in parking lots and residential driveways. Sadly, the driver backing up is usually blamed for such accidents. This is another reason why you should back up your vehicle with caution.

22. The correct answer is: (B). Inspecting your environment while backing up.

The GOAL approach simply means "get out and look." The approach underscores the significance of checking your surroundings while backing up. When you have a good idea of your environment, you can easily avoid potholes, blind spots and other potential problems.

23. The correct answer is: (B). Someone who checks your environment for potential obstacles while backing up.

Sometimes, you may need someone to check your surroundings when you are behind the wheel. The spotter will inform you of potential problems. With effective communication between both of you, a spotter is an asset.

24. The correct answer is: (A). Twice.

Before you start backing up, tap your horn twice to notify other road users or passersby and avoid preventable accidents. The horn will draw people's attention to your vehicle as well as enable them to know the direction you are coming from. This can come in handy in crowded areas.

25. The correct answer is: (B). Rear-vision cameras.

With the cameras, you can see your vehicle's rear easily and avoid running into obstacles. Hence, your problems with rear blind spots are solved once you have full visual control of your vehicle's rear while backing up.

Doubles and Triples Test 1 – 25 Questions

1. What are doubles and triples?
    a. Long vehicles with two or more trailers attached to the truck's tractor.
    b. Long vehicles with a trailer or two attached to the truck's tractor.
    c. Long vehicles with two or more truck tractors.
    d. Long vehicles with more than two truck tractors.

2. Doubles and triples are also known as ...
    a. Longer Commercial Vehicles.
    b. Longer Combination Vehicles.
    c. Large Commercial Vehicles.
    d. Large Combination Vehicles.

3. Do states have common restrictions on triples?
    a. Yes.
    b. No.
    c. It depends on the type of triples.
    d. It depends on the type of license a driver holds.

4. What does an assembly procedure entail?
    a. It is a test of your ability to assemble a vehicle from scratch.
    b. It is a test of your ability to fix whatever you uncouple.
    c. It is a test of your ability to operate vehicles driven directly from assembly plants.
    d. It is a test of whether you meet vehicle assembling requirements or not.

5. What is a test of your ability to operate a vehicle irrespective of potential challenges?
    a. Handling procedure.
    b. Handling requirements.
    c. Handling.
    d. Handling problem solutions.

6. To take the Doubles and Triples test you must pay a:
    a. Licensing fee.
    b. Testing fee.
    c. None of the above.
    d. All of the above.

7. Your choice of test location is dependent on several factors that include ...
    a. Your state of residence.
    b. The type of double or triple you drive.
    c. Your license type.
    d. Your learner's permit.

8. One of the most common problems associated with pulling doubles or triples is ...
    a. Their weight.
    b. They are too long.
    c. They are less stable than other vehicles.
    d. All of the above.

9. What is a preventive measure against rolling over in doubles or triples?
    a. Carrying fewer loads.
    b. Driving slowly.
    c. Steering gently.
    d. Both B and C.

10. The crack-the-whip effect usually occurs when ...
    a. A trailer driver applies the brakes suddenly.
    b. A trailer driver changes lane quickly.
    c. The trailer is overloaded.
    d. The driver increases the driving speed suddenly.

11. It is advisable to leave space between you and the vehicle ahead of you. Why?
    a. To enable your vehicle to turn suddenly.
    b. To make it easier for you to overtake the vehicle ahead.
    c. To allow smaller vehicles to overtake your trailer easily.
    d. To make it easier to maneuver your vehicle.

12. ... and ... are problems common to doubles and triples when mountain driving.
    a. Skidding and loss of traction.
    b. Loss of traction and jackknifing.
    c. Skidding and careless overtaking.
    d. All of the above.

13. One of several factors you must consider when parking is ...
    a. Ease of driving out of the parking lot.
    b. Ease of driving into the parking lot.
    c. Ease of using the brakes when necessary.
    d. Ease of managing bad weather.

14. An important step towards ensuring your trailer's emergency brakes function properly is ...
    a. Securing the trailer.
    b. Oiling the emergency brakes.
    c. Connecting the emergency brakes with a fifth-wheel dolly.
    d. Chocking the wheels.

15. The semitrailer with the heaviest load should be connected ...
    a. In front of the tractor.
    b. Behind the tractor.
    c. Behind other semitrailers.
    d. Wherever you are comfortable.

16. Where is the most appropriate location for the converter dolly?
    a. In front of the main first trailer.
    b. In front of the tractor.
    c. Beside the rear trailer.
    d. In front of the rear trailer.

17. How do you connect the first semitrailer to the converter dolly?
    a. By locking the pintle hood and securing the converter gear support.
    b. By directly locking the pintle hood and converter dolly.
    c. By connecting them through a connector hook.
    d. Using a specially designed converter connector.

18. During a trailer coupling, there shouldn't be spaces between the ... and ...
    a. Lower and upper fifth wheel.
    b. Converter dolly and kingpin.
    c. Safety chains and light cords.
    d. Air tank petcock and first trailer.

19. How do you charge the brakes?
    a. By applying more pressure to the brake pad.
    b. By reducing pressure to the brake pad.
    c. By pushing the air supply knob in.
    d. By shutting the valves off.

20. What are the most important benefits of inspecting your vehicle regularly?
    a. It makes the vehicle safer to drive.
    b. It saves time.
    c. It satisfies your conscience.
    d. All of the above.

21. Where can you take the doubles and triples test?
    a. At a third-party site.
    b. At the local Department of Motor Vehicles.
    c. All of the above.
    d. None of the above.

22. What does LCV stand for?
    a. Longer Commercial Vehicle.
    b. Longer Communication Vehicle.
    c. Larger Combination Vehicles.
    d. Longer Combination Vehicles.

23. The doubles and triples test covers all of the following except:
    a. Assembly procedures.
    b. Potential problems.
    c. Handling.
    d. Purchasing and supply.

24. All of the following factors make operating a double or triple trailer more challenging except:
    a. The cost of purchase.
    b. Its sheer size.
    c. Its outstanding weight.
    d. The incredible length.

25. While uncoupling the rear trailer, you must take the following precautions:
    a. Park the rig on level and firm ground.
    b. Park the rig in a straight line.
    c. Remove some of its load.
    d. All of the above.

Doubles and Triples Test 1 Answers

1. The correct answer is: (A). These are long vehicles with two or more trailers attached to the truck's tractor.

Although there are different types of combination vehicles, the doubles and triples stand out. In the former, two trailers are attached to the truck's tractor while three or more trailers are attached to the tractor in the latter.

2. The correct answer is: (C). Large Commercial Vehicles.

Double and triple trailers are otherwise known as Longer Commercial Vehicles. It is apparent from their names that this set of vehicles is longer, bigger and weighs more than other vehicles in the commercial vehicle class. Thus, this class of vehicle requires extra driving skills to operate.

3. The correct answer is: (B). No.

States don't have a consensus agreement on restrictions on triples. Each state defines its own rules that govern combination vehicles, triples inclusive. Thus, it is imperative that you are familiar with the rules and regulations governing the activities of commercial vehicle operators in your state of residence.

4. The correct answer is: (B). It is a test of your ability to fix whatever you uncouple.

Sometimes, you may need to uncouple your vehicle, either to detect a problem or fix one. If you can't re-couple the vehicle, you run the risk of operating a badly coupled vehicle, which is a time bomb.

5. The correct answer is: (C). Handling.

Handling is a test of your ability to operate a vehicle irrespective of the potential challenges. Since driving is not always without occasional challenges, your ability to handle these problems will enhance your driving skills.

6. The correct answer is: (C). None of the above.

When applying for the test, you must pay a testing fee and licensing fee. Your state may also require some additional fees.

7. The correct answer is: (A). Your state of residence.

Since drivers take the test in their location of choice and states have different requirements, you have a better chance of meeting the requirements of your state of residence than somewhere you are not familiar with.

8. The correct answer is: (C). They are less stable than other vehicles.

When driving doubles or triples, you have to consider their instability. They are notably less stable than other vehicles, one of the reasons why they are prone to rolling over, jackknifing and other related problems.

9. The correct answer is: (D). Both B and C. Driving slowly and steering gently.

Rolling over is common to long vehicles. It occurs when the vehicle loses balance and rolls over, perhaps due to speeding or abrupt steering control. You can prevent this by driving slowly and steering gently.

10. The correct answer is: (B). When a trailer driver changes lanes quickly.

The crack-the-whip effect usually occurs when a trailer driver changes lane quickly. The tractor and the attached trailers will feel the effect of the abrupt lane change differently. While a section of the vehicle may not feel the impact too much, another part may feel it, leading to rollover.

11. The correct answer is: (D). To make it easier for the driver to maneuver the vehicle.

Long vehicles are usually more difficult to maneuver than their shorter counterparts. Hence, you must consider this factor when driving. Don't follow a vehicle so closely that you find it challenging to avoid an accident.

12. The correct answer is: (A). Skidding and loss of traction.

Two problems that are common to doubles and triples are skidding and loss of traction. They are responsible for most of the accidents involving this type of vehicle. Sudden brake application can cause skidding, which invariably causes jackknifing too.

13. The correct answer is: (A). Ease of driving out of the parking lot.

When parking a long vehicle, consider the ease of driving out of the parking lot. Unlike with smaller vehicles, you need plenty of space.

14. The correct answer is: (A). Securing the trailer.

An important step towards ensuring your trailer's emergency brakes function properly is securing the rear trailer.

15. The correct answer is: (B). Behind the tractor.

The semitrailer with the heaviest load should be connected behind the tractor. In that position, it is easier to pull the trailer. More so, it offers the combination vehicle the needed stability that will prevent it from jackknifing or rolling over when in motion.

16. The correct answer is: (D). In front of the rear trailer.

The best place to put the converter dolly is in front of the rear trailer. In this position, it is able to connect the tractor and trailer with relative ease. This contributes significantly to the overall stability of the vehicle.

17. The correct answer is: (A). By locking the pintle hood and securing the converter gear support.

Place the first semitrailer in front of the converter dolly and hook it to the front trailer by locking the pintle hook and securing the converter gear support while in a raised position.

18. The correct answer is: (A). Lower and upper fifth wheel.

While coupling your trailer, ensure that there are no spaces between the lower and upper fifth wheel. The locking jaws should also be closed on the kingpin before connecting the air hoses, safety chains and light cords. Once you are done with that, close the air tank petcock.

19. The correct answer is: (C). By pushing the air supply knob in.

You can charge the brakes by pushing the air supply knob in. Once you are done with that, you can check the second trailer for air by opening the emergency line shutoff. If there is no air pressure, the brakes won't work.

20. The correct answer is: (A). It makes the vehicle safer to drive.

There are several benefits to carrying out routine inspections on your vehicle. In general, such regular inspections help you to identify and fix potential problems before they get out of hand.

21. The correct answer is: (C). All of the above.

You can take the test either at the local DMV or a third-party site. While some states are comfortable with third-party sites, others make it mandatory that the tests are done via the department. Hence, your state of residence will play a huge role in your choice.

22. The correct answer is: (D). Longer Combination Vehicles.

LCV stands for Longer Combination Vehicles. It is a collection of vehicles that are not only bigger than other vehicles, but also longer and heavier as well. In this group are tankers, heavy school buses, large vehicles for transporting hazardous materials and a host of others.

23. The correct answer is: (D). Purchasing and supply.

When taking the doubles and triples test, your examiner will test your knowledge of handling, assembly procedures and potential problems. Note, however, that it is at each state's discretion to choose the format and style of the exam. While the general concept remains the same, the content may differ.

24. The correct answer is: (A). The cost of purchase.

While double or triple trailers are undoubtedly expensive, that doesn't impact a driver's ability to operate them. However, their sheer size, length and outstanding weight can make them a handful for most drivers. These factors also underscore the need for competent drivers to handle them, hence the need for this test.

25. The correct answer is: (D). All of the above.

These are some safety precautions you should take into consideration when uncoupling the rear trailer. Removing some of its load makes it lighter and easier to uncouple. Parking the rig on level and firm ground prevents the vehicle from accidentally rolling forward or backward, which is the same reason for parking it in a straight line.

Tanker Test 1 – 25 Questions

1. The ... regulates the activities of tanker drivers across the United States.
    a. Federal Motor Carrier Safety Administration.
    b. Federal Motor Safety Administration.
    c. Federal Motor Company Security Administration.
    d. Federal Motor Security Administration.

2. The FMCSA is an arm of the ...
    a. United States Department of Security and Health.
    b. United States Department of Transportation.
    c. United States Department of Road Safety.
    d. United States Department of Transportation and Road Safety.

3. The FMCSA's primary mission is to ...
    a. Reduce the number of tanker drivers across the country.
    b. Reduce vehicle-related accidents in the United States.
    c. Control the operation of tanks.
    d. All of the above.

4. The FMCSA outlaws the ...
    a. Transportation of a significant quantity of liquids or gases without the right training and endorsement.
    b. Transportation of goods across the country in a commercial vehicle.
    c. Driving of commercial vehicles above a certain age.
    d. All of the above.

5. The term "tanker" covers all of the following vehicles except:
    a. Box trucks.
    b. Flatbeds.
    c. Reefers.
    d. Armored tanks.

6. One of the conditions for a CDL with a tanker endorsement is ...
    a. You must only drive empty tankers.
    b. The tanker must be loaded.
    c. It must be a six-wheel tanker.
    d. The tanker's container must have the capacity to carry over 500 gallons.

7. It is illegal to carry over ... gallons of liquid in the container.
    a. 2,000.
    b. 5,000.
    c. 8,000.
    d. 10,000.

8. One of the exceptions to the above rule is that the trailer must ...
    a. Be a new trailer.
    b. Be driven by a driver with over five years of driving experience.
    c. Be a temporary attachment to a flatbed trailer.
    d. All of the above.

9. Under what condition can you drive a tanker with a Commercial Learner's Permit?
    a. The tank must be empty.
    b. You must have a tank endorsement on the CLP.
    c. The tank must be cleaned and purged if it has been used for transporting hazardous materials in the past.
    d. All of the above.

10. Some of the factors that determine the quantity of liquid you can carry with a tanker are:
    a. Load temperature and the liquid's expansion rate.
    b. The liquid's expansion rate and cost of transportation.
    c. Load temperature and viscosity.
    d. None of the above.

11. What is GCWR?
    a. Gross Container Weight Record.
    b. Gross Container Weight Rating.
    c. Gross Combination Weight Record.
    d. Gross Combination Weight Rating.

12. Some tankers can't be fully loaded. Why?
    a. They are specifically designed that way.
    b. They increase in volume during transportation.
    c. They are at their maximum weight limit in their half-full state.
    d. All of the above.

13. The tanker regulations to effect across the United States in ...
    a. March 2007.
    b. March 2017.
    c. March 2015.
    d. March 2012.

14. The penalty for violating tanker regulations is ...
    a. $500.
    b. $1,000.
    c. $2,000.
    d. $5,000.

15. You may be suspended for ... if you are caught violating the rules for operating a tanker.
    a. 15 days.
    b. 30 days.
    c. 10 days.
    d. 90 days.

16. Rollovers are common in tankers due to their ...
    a. Poor steering.
    b. Bad wheels.
    c. High center of gravity.
    d. None of the above.

17. A common problem tanker drivers must contend with is ...
    a. Bouncing heads.
    b. Bulkheads.
    c. Bolt heads.
    d. Bald heads.

18. The movement of a tanker's contents from one side to another is called ...
    a. Surging head.
    b. Bulkhead.
    c. Surge.
    d. Bolt head.

19. Spreading the weight of a tanker's load is a solution to ...
    a. Bulkhead.
    b. Surge.
    c. Contamination.
    d. Rollover.

20. The tanker endorsement test covers a wide range of areas that include all of the following except:
    a. Maintenance.
    b. Safety procedures.
    c. Loading and offloading.
    d. Inspection.

21. Are tanker drivers permitted to carry any quantity of liquid?
    a. It's at the driver's discretion.
    b. No.
    c. Yes.
    d. It depends on several factors.

22. The FMCSA was established on ...
    a. December 25, 2006.
    b. January 15, 2001.
    c. January 1, 2000.
    d. March 10, 2002.

23. The ... emphasized the importance of road safety measures prior to the enactment of the FMCSA.
    a. Motor Safety Improvement Act.
    b. Motor Carrier Safety Improvement Commission.
    c. Motor Carrier Safety Improvement Act.
    d. Motor Carrier and Safety Improvement Commission.

24. Does the type of content you transport with the tanker count in favor of or against you during the test?
    a. It sometimes counts against you.
    b. No.
    c. Yes.
    d. It always counts in favor of you.

25. When can surge trigger rollover?
    a. When driving on sand.
    b. When driving on a watery road.
    c. When driving on ice.
    d. When driving an empty tank.

Tanker Test 1 Answers

1. The correct answer is: (A). Federal Motor Carrier Safety Administration.

The Federal Motor Carrier Safety Administration is responsible for regulating the activities of tanker drivers across the United States.

2. The correct answer is: (B). United States Department of Transportation.

The FMCSA is under the supervision of the United States Department of Transportation. This department's primary mission is to reduce the number of injuries caused by large buses and trucks.

3. The correct answer is: (B). Reduce vehicle-related accidents in the United States.

The FMCSA's primary mission is to reduce vehicle-related accidents and fatalities caused by large buses and trucks in the United States.

4. The correct answer is: (A). Transportation of a significant quantity of liquids or gases without the right training and endorsement.

For reasons of safety, the FMCSA places restrictions on the transportation of liquids and gases across the country with a tanker.

5. The correct answer is: (D). Armored tanks.

The term "tanker" covers a wide range of vehicles. This includes box trucks, flatbeds, dry vans and reefers. The FMCSA stipulates that if you drive any of these vehicles, you must have the right endorsement on your CDL.

6. The correct answer is: (B). The tanker must be loaded.

There are certain conditions under which your CDL must be accompanied by a tanker endorsement. One such condition is that the tanker *must* be fully loaded.

7. The correct answer is: (D). 10,000.

A tanker driver can't carry over 10,000 gallons of liquid. This prevents accidents due to overloading and other related mistakes.

8. The correct answer is: (C). Be a temporary attachment to a flatbed trailer.

You don't need a special endorsement to operate a temporary attachment to a flatbed trailer, to operate a tank designed for transporting goods or an empty tank.

9. The correct answer is: (D). All of the above.

You can operate a tanker with a Commercial Learner's Permit under certain conditions such as if the tank is empty or if you have a tank endorsement on the permit. If the tank has previously been used to transport hazardous materials, you must clean and purge it.

10. The correct answer is: (A). Load temperature and the liquid's expansion rate.

Restrictions are placed on the quantity of liquid a tanker can transport at a time. Some of the factors that determine the quantity include load temperature and the liquid's expansion rate. Other factors are the maximum weight limit allowed by the government on public roads and the tank's volume capacity.

11. The correct answer is: (D). Gross Combination Weight Rating.

GCWR means Gross Combination Weight Rating. This refers to the maximum allowed combined mass of a combination vehicle which includes both the cargo and the passengers. For a tanker, this is the combined mass of the passengers in the tanker as well as the tank's contents.

12. The correct answer is: (C). They are at their maximum weight limit in their half-full state.

Some loads reach the maximum weight limit, even before the tank is filled up. In such cases, the tank can't be fully loaded. Thus, the tank will have some extra space that can cause a problem while transporting liquids.

13. The correct answer is: (B). March 2017.

In an attempt to regulate the trucking industry, especially the tanker subsector, the government introduced the tanker regulations in March 2017. Since then, it is mandatory for tanker drivers to meet some basic requirements before they are deemed qualified to operate a tanker. Violators are seriously penalized.

14. The correct answer is: (D).$5,000.

In order to enforce the rules and regulations, the regulatory body fines tanker drivers without the right authorization to operate such vehicles $5,000. This is to serve as a deterrent to others and serve as a warning to others of the FMSCA's zero tolerance of violations of its regulations.

15. The correct answer is: (D). 90 days.

Aside from the monetary penalty of $5,000, you may also face a long suspension time of 90 days.

16. The correct answer is: (C). A high center of gravity.

Rollovers are common in tankers because, unlike smaller vehicles, they have a very high center of gravity. Thus, they are highly unstable and can be affected by conditions such as driving on ice, an abrupt lane change and bad weather.

17. The correct answer is: (B). Bulkheads.

One of the biggest challenges a tanker driver must contend with is bulkhead-related problems. A bulkhead is a barrier or a dividing wall between the compartments in the tank. Bulkheads are used for dividing large tanks into smaller tanks. They make the effects of a surge more pronounced in tankers.

18. The correct answer is: (C). Surge.

The movement of a tanker's contents from one side to another is known as surge. Surge is common when a tanker is stopped. The liquid will move forward in response to the stop action and hit the front of the tank, shoving the tank forward and vice versa.

19. The correct answer is: (A). Bulkhead.

Since bulkhead is triggered by the existence of dividing walls in a tanker, the problem can be addressed by spreading the weight of the tanker's load evenly among the compartments. This will prevent the bulkhead from affecting the tanker adversely.

20. The correct answer is: (C). Loading and offloading.

The tanker endorsement test covers a wide range of areas that include maintenance, safety procedures and inspection.

21. The correct answer is: (B). No.

Drivers can transport gaseous or liquid containers that can carry more than 119 gallons. The total volume of the containers' content exceeds 1,000 gallons.

22. The correct answer is: (C). January 1, 2000.

The FMCSA was established on January 1, 2000, pursuant to the Motor Carrier Safety Improvement Act of 1999.

23. The correct answer is: (C). The Motor Carrier Safety Improvement Act.

The Motor Carrier Safety Improvement Act emphasized the importance of road safety measures prior to the enactment of the FMCSA.

24. The correct answer is: (B). No.

While several factors count towards your eligibility for the test, the type of content you carry isn't one of them. The focus is on meeting other requirements as stipulated by the regulatory body.

25. The correct answer is: (C). When driving on ice.

Rollover is more often than not triggered by ice. Thus, when driving on ice, you should take extra care, drive slowly and steer carefully.

Passenger Transport Test 1 – 25 Questions

1. The minimum number of people a passenger vehicle can transport is ...
    a. 20 people.
    b. 15 people.
    c. 16 people.
    d. 25 people.

2. The P Endorsement is for operators of all of the following types of vehicles except:
    a. Service buses for factories and church buses.
    b. Taxis.
    c. Buses.
    d. All of the above.

3. Another important test you must pass is the ...
    a. Safety Endorsement Test.
    b. Security Endorsement Test.
    c. Loading Endorsement Test.
    d. Air Brakes Endorsement Test.

4. Under what conditions can you use a passenger vehicle's emergency exit?
    a. During a fire.
    b. After a crash.
    c. During incidents that can cause injuries or loss of life.
    d. All of the above.

5. When is it advisable to consider an alternative to evacuation?
    a. During a crash.
    b. During a collision that leads to a loss of life.
    c. During a fire.
    d. During incidents that don't lead to a loss of life or serious injuries.

6. The FMSCA recommends testing a passenger vehicle's emergency exit every ...
    a. 50 days.
    b. 30 days.
    c. 60 days.
    d. 90 days.

7. When is it appropriate to show passengers the emergency exit?
    a. During a fire.
    b. Prior to a crash.
    c. At your convenience.
    d. As soon as you are ready to start driving.

8. What is the first step during an emergency?
    a. Evacuate the passengers without delay.
    b. Conduct a row-by-row evacuation.
    c. Alternate evacuating the sides of the bus.
    d. Inform the passengers of the need for evacuation.

9. Is it advisable to keep the emergency exit locked if passengers are aboard?
    a. Yes.
    b. No.
    c. It doesn't matter.
    d. It's based on personal preference.

10. Under what conditions should you keep the emergency exit locked while in transit?
    a. When transporting people in police custody.
    b. When contracted by law enforcement agencies.
    c. All of the above
    d. None of the above.

11. Why is it advisable to direct the passengers to a safe place during an emergency?
    a. For easy accountability.
    b. For convenience.
    c. For no real reason.
    d. A and B.

12. A minimum of ... driving experience is required to be eligible for a passenger bus license.
    a. Three years'.
    b. Five years'.
    c. Four years'.
    d. Ten years'.

13. Which of the following will disqualify you from taking the passenger transport test?
    a. Previous conviction of acts of terrorism.
    b. Previous conviction of driving under the influence.
    c. None of the above.
    d. All of the above.

14. Why is conversing with a passenger not advisable while driving?
    a. It makes the passenger more abusive.
    b. You lose your self-respect.
    c. You may be distracted.
    d. B and C.

15. Under what conditions should you not refuel your vehicle?
    a. In closed buildings.
    b. When passengers are on board.
    c. None of the above.
    d. All of the above.

16. When should you inspect your vehicle?
    a. Before a trip.
    b. After a trip.
    c. Both before and after a trip.
    d. At your convenience.

17. ... drivers are required to write up a formal inspection report after each trip.
    a. Interstate drivers.
    b. Intrastate drivers.
    c. Independent drivers.
    d. New drivers.

18. How does the brake-door interlock work?
    a. It is remotely controlled by the driver.
    b. It automatically engages when the door opens.
    c. It opens and closes at will.
    d. It allows the driver to stop the vehicle without using the traditional brakes.

19. The brake-door interlock complements the efforts of the ...
    a. Parking brake system.
    b. Emergency brake system.
    c. Traditional brake system.
    d. All of the above.

20. It is unwise to ... when using the brake-lock interlock.
    a. Apply the parking brake.
    b. Apply the emergency brake.
    c. Take your foot off the brake pedal.
    d. Switch off the lock remotely.

21. A safe oil level is when the gauge is between ... and ...
    a. Full and add levels.
    b. Add and full levels.
    c. Intermediate and full levels.
    d. Intermediate and add levels.

22. A functional power steering system should not be ...
    a. Leaking when parked.
    b. Leaking when in use.
    c. Leaking when tightly screwed.
    d. A and C.

23. A functional alternator has a tension level between ... and ...
    a. ½ inch and ¾ inch.
    b. 2/3 inch and 4/5 inch.
    c. ½ inch and 2/5 inch.
    d. 2/5 inch and 3/5 inch.

24. A good air compressor must:
    a. Have sufficient air pressure and the belt mustn't be frayed.
    b. Be well lubricated and have enough air pressure.
    c. Not be frayed or well lubricated.
    d. Have sufficient air pressure and a frayed belt.

25. To qualify for the P endorsement, an applicant must be at least ...
    a. 18 years old.
    b. 21 years old.
    c. 30 years old.
    d. 35 years old.

Passenger Transport Test 1 Answers

1. The correct answer is: (C). 16 people.

A passenger vehicle should carry a minimum of 16 passengers, including the driver.

2. The correct answer is: (D). All of the above.

The P Endorsement is a special type of endorsement for operators who desire to operate a wide range of vehicles that include service buses for factories, church buses, general buses and taxis.

3. The correct answer is: (D). Air Brakes Endorsement Test.

Most large vehicles, including passenger buses, are equipped with an air brake system. Thus, in addition to passing the general passenger bus test, you must also take a special air brakes test. This is to ensure that you are familiar with the operation of the brake system.

4. The correct answer is: (D). All of the above.

The emergency exit is designed for use in emergency situations only. It should be used in conjunction with the regular exit.

5. The correct answer is: (D). Incidents that don't lead to a loss of life or serious injuries.

While evacuation may be the best solution in some cases, some exceptional cases warrant the consideration of other alternatives. For instance, there isn't a need for evacuation if an incident doesn't lead to serious injuries or a loss of life.

6. The correct answer is: (D). 90 days.

According to the FMSCA, each driver should test the emergency exits every 90 days. This is to identify possible issues with the exits and keep them in full working order.

7. The correct answer is: (D). As soon as you are ready to start driving.

It is good practice to inform the passengers of the existence of emergency exits and their locations at the start of a trip, before any emergency may present itself.

8. The correct answer is: (D). Inform the passengers of the need for evacuation.

When an emergency situation arises, don't panic. Reassure your passengers of their safety. If you must evacuate them, explain your decision. Inform them of the need for the evacuation and share safety precautions they should take.

9. The correct answer is: (B). No.

It is not advisable to keep the emergency exit locked when passengers are on board. This may make it difficult to use the exits when emergency situations arise.

10. The correct answer is: (C). All of the above.

Although the rule of thumb suggests the emergency exit door shouldn't be locked when passengers are on board, there are some exceptions. For instance, you should keep exits locked when transporting people in police custody or when contracted by law enforcement agencies.

11. The correct answer is: (A). For easy accountability.

During an emergency such as a car crash, some passengers may get lost in the chaos. It is easier to know those who are missing if you direct the other passengers to a safe place. This enables the driver or other people to search for the missing passengers.

12. The correct answer is: (A). Three years.

You must have a minimum of three years of experience to operate a passenger vehicle. This is for your safety, the safety of the passengers and the safety of other road users.

13. The correct answer is: (D). All of the above.

Even if you meet the eligibility requirements for the license, you may still be denied the license under some conditions such as if you have been convicted of acts of terrorism or of driving under the influence of drugs or alcohol.

14. The correct answer is: (C). You may be distracted.

Distraction is the primary reason behind this restriction. Focusing on the road may be difficult when you are engaged in a serious discussion with a passenger. Your inability to pay undivided attention to the road endangers your life, that of your passengers and other road users as well.

15. The correct answer is: (D). All of the above.

Don't refuel in closed buildings or when passengers are on board your vehicle to prevent them from exposure to poisonous fuel vapors.

16. The correct answer is: (C). Before and after a trip.

It is necessary that you inspect the vehicle regularly, both pre- and post-trip, to enable you to identify potential problems and fix them before they get out of hand.

17. The correct answer is: (A). Interstate drivers.

Interstate drivers are required to write up a formal post-trip inspection report after each trip and submit it to their employer. The report must include vehicle type and any observations made during the inspection such as whether there are damaged parts that need to be replaced.

18. The correct answer is: (B). It automatically engages when the door opens.

The brake-door interlock is an automatic braking system that becomes fully operational whenever the door opens. It keeps the vehicle stationary while passengers are alighting. This is an effective preventive measure against accidents that occur when passengers are getting off a bus.

19. The correct answer is: (A). Parking brake system.

The brake-door interlock complements the parking brake system since it also helps keep the stopped vehicle stationary once the vehicle's doors are opened.

20. The correct answer is: (C). Take the foot off the brake pedal.

Some drivers erroneously consider the brake-door interlock a replacement for the parking brake. They take their foot off the brake pedal once the interlock is engaged. This is dangerous as the interlock disengages automatically when the door closes. The interlock complements the parking brake's efforts. It does not replace it.

21. The correct answer is: (B). Add and full levels.

When checking the oil level, it is good to know that the oil level is safe for use when it is between the add and full level. If it is below the correct level, top up the oil before driving. Otherwise, you may be taking a huge risk with the engine.

22. The correct answer is: (C). Leaking when screwed tight.

A check of your power steering system is also recommended during your pre- and post-trip inspection. If the power steering is functional and is in good condition, it shouldn't be leaking when screwed tight. If it does, you must identify the issue and fix it without delay.

23. The correct answer is: (A). ½ inch and ¾ inch.

Pay attention to the alternator during the inspection. When it is performing at maximum capacity, its tension level should be between ½ inch and ¾ inch. Any reading besides this is an indication of any error somewhere that needs urgent attention.

24. The correct answer is: (A). Must have sufficient air pressure and the belt mustn't be frayed.

The air compressor, as an important passenger bus component, must have sufficient pressure to perform its duties. Otherwise, it may malfunction. Its belt is another area that deserves attention. It mustn't be frayed or broken.

25. The correct answer is: (B). 21 years.

Until you are 21, you won't qualify for the passenger bus endorsement. This is to ensure that only people that are legally considered adults are permitted to drive such vehicles.

School Bus Test 1 – 25 Questions

1. Before you are considered eligible to drive a school bus, you must pass the ...
    a. School Bus Management Test.
    b. School Bus Driving Test.
    c. School Bus Endorsement Test.
    d. School Bus Driving and Endorsement Test.

2. Before you become a school bus driver, you must ...
    a. Receive practical instruction pertaining to school bus driving.
    b. Have customer service skills.
    c. Understand the rules and regulations guiding school bus driving.
    d. All of the above.

3. Which of the following medical reports are you required to present in order to be eligible to drive a school bus?
    a. A Medical Examiner's Certificate.
    b. A Comprehensive Medical Examiner's Certificate.
    c. A Medical Examination Certificate.
    d. A Comprehensive Medical Examination Certificate.

4. How often must you submit the required certificate?
    a. Every five years.
    b. Every three years.
    c. Annually.
    d. Every two years.

5. What is the significance of the medical test?
    a. To teach you how to handle medical emergencies while driving.
    b. To ensure you are physically and mentally competent to handle the job.
    c. To prepare you to communicate with customers.
    d. To improve your marketability.

6. When are students more prone to accidents in school buses?
    a. When taking a selfie inside the bus.
    b. During the loading stage.
    c. During the unloading stage.
    d. During both the loading and the unloading stages.

7. When are students most at risk?
    a. While inside school buses.
    b. While getting on or off school buses.
    c. While walking towards school buses.
    d. While walking away from school buses.

8. The danger zone refers to the ...
    a. Areas where students are picked up or dropped off from the school bus.
    b. The areas where students are taken during emergencies.
    c. The areas around the vehicle where students are more prone to accidents.
    d. None of the above.

9. What effect does the danger zone have on drivers?
    a. It makes them sleepy.
    b. The driver's vision may be blocked.
    c. It makes them more forgetful.
    d. It impairs their sense of hearing and speech.

10. Define the blind spot.
    a. This is somewhere around the school bus where accident rates are high.
    b. It refers to 10 feet on either side of the vehicle where the driver is obstructed.
    c. It refers to areas behind the school bus with obstructed visibility.
    d. All of the above.

11. The regulatory body that recommends special training for drivers is the ...
    a. National Council for Drivers' Awareness.
    b. Department of School Transportation.
    c. National Safety Council.
    d. National Department of School Transportation and Safety.

12. The factors that must be considered when considering the best training program in a state include ...
    a. The federal government's stance on school bus driving.
    b. Each school's needs.
    c. Each driver's individual circumstances.
    d. All of the above.

13. A safe distance for activating the warning flasher system is ...
    a. 50 feet before the stop zone.
    b. 10 feet before the stop zone.
    c. 200 feet before the stop zone.
    d. 100 feet before the stop zone.

14. Picking up and dropping off should be done at ...
    a. Convenient spots for the students.
    b. Convenient spots for the driver.
    c. Designated drop-off and pick-up points.
    d. A and C.

15. The safest place for students to cross the road after drop-off is ...
    a. In front of the school bus.
    b. Behind the school bus.
    c. Anywhere around the school bus.
    d. Wherever the students choose.

16. Check all of the following places except ... when leaving the drop-off point.
    a. All side mirrors.
    b. Crossover for approaching students.
    c. Crossover for exiting students.
    d. None of the above.

17. Why must you talk a walk through the bus after completing a route?
    a. You don't need to.
    b. To check for sleeping students and forgotten articles.
    c. To check for acts of vandalism.
    d. Both B and C.

18. What steps must you take before you open the school bus door for loading or unloading?
    a. Put the vehicle in neutral and engage the parking brake.
    b. Put the vehicle in neutral and engage the emergency brake.
    c. Put the vehicle in neutral and engage the interlocks.
    d. Put the vehicle in neutral and engage the emergency blinkers.

19. For additional safety, what should you do before you move your vehicle after unloading or loading?
    a. Silence the passengers.
    b. Look for signs of approaching students or vehicles.
    c. Turn off your radio and other noisy equipment.
    d. Both A and C.

20. Which of the following items can cause an accident in the bus' doorway?
    a. A book bag.
    b. Jacket straps.
    c. A backpack.
    d. All of the above.

21. When is it advisable to give students some practical safety tips?
    a. At the beginning of the school season only.
    b. Towards the end of the school season.
    c. At the beginning and throughout the school season.
    d. At the beginning and the middle of the school season.

22. Picking students up at corners shortly before making a right turn is ...
    a. A safe driving habit.
    b. Something that exposes you and your passengers to risks.
    c. A skill that should be practiced until mastered.
    d. A criminal offense.

23. What should you do after each trip?
    a. Park the vehicle on the school's premises and go home.
    b. Conduct a post-trip inspection.
    c. Close the windows and doors and park the vehicle in the school's garage.
    d. Do whatever is convenient for you.

24. During a post-trip inspection, inspect all of the following bus parts except:
    a. The stop signal arms.
    b. The warning lights.
    c. The mirror systems.
    d. None of the above.

25. When you notice something out of place during an inspection, what should you do?

    a. Notify law enforcement immediately.
    b. Notify your supervisor or the school immediately.
    c. Fix the problems before parking the vehicle.
    d. Record your observation and keep the record for future reference.

School Bus Test 1 Answers

1. The correct answer is: (C). School Bus Endorsement Test.

Before you are considered eligible to operate a school bus, your examiner must be convinced of your ability to handle the bus safely. Hence, it is mandatory that you take the School Bus Endorsement Test and pass it before your endorsement is confirmed.

2. The correct answer is: (D). All of the above.

Before you can be endorsed to drive a school bus you must be trained in customer service skills, practical instructions about school bus driving and understanding the rules and regulations guiding the operation of school buses. Once you are done with the program, you can take the test.

3. The correct answer is: (A). A Medical Examiner's Certificate.

As proof of your physical fitness, you are required to provide a Medical Examiner's Certificate as proof of your eligibility for the license.

4. The correct answer is: (D). Every two years.

Apart from providing the Medical Examiner's Certificate before you are licensed, you must also resubmit it every two years. This is primarily to ensure that you still maintain the physical and mental fitness that initially qualified you for the license. If your mental or physical health deteriorates, your endorsement may be withdrawn.

5. The correct answer is: (B). To ensure you are physically and mentally competent to handle the job.

Driving is both physically and mentally challenging. Loading and unloading, and stopping at different drop-off and pick-up points may test your physical fitness. Thus, a potential employer may be concerned about your ability to meet the challenges and will test them accordingly.

6. The correct answer is: (D). During loading and unloading.

Students are more prone to accidents while being dropped off by a school bus or when boarding it. This is especially true if the aisle is obstructed or school bags or other items get caught in the doorway. Sometimes, a student may be hit while in the blind spot too.

7. The correct answer is: (B). While getting on or off school buses.

Students are vulnerable to accidents when boarding or alighting from school buses. There are reportedly more deaths at such times than those that occur while inside school buses.

8. The correct answer is: (C). The areas around the vehicle where students are more prone to accidents.

These are areas where the driver's vision is blocked so he/she may not be able to see the boarding or exiting students clearly. Such areas include blind spots ten feet on either side of the vehicle and in front of the vehicle.

9. The correct answer is: (B). The driver's vision may be blocked.

Drivers are more vulnerable to accidents in the danger zone. This can lead to making a wrong driving decision that may trigger a crash or other accidents.

10. The correct answer is: (D). All of the above.

Blind spots are areas behind the school bus where drivers have obstructed visibility. These are areas around the school bus which are more prone to accidents.

11. The correct answer is: (C). National Safety Council.

The National Safety Council recommends special training for school bus drivers to ensure the safety of students, drivers, pedestrians, etc.

12. The correct answer is: (C). The driver's individual situation.

The basic requirements for eligibility for a school bus endorsement differ from state to state. Hence, each state must consider the individual needs of potential drivers.

13. The correct answer is: (D). 100 feet before the stop zone.

Before stopping the vehicle, notify other drivers of your intention by activating the warning light system. It's best to activate the system 100 feet before the stop zone. This helps you to avoid dangerously abrupt stops.

14. The correct answer is: (C). Designated drop-off and pick-up points.

Only drop off and pick up students at designated points. This not only makes it easier to discharge your duties but is safer and less time-consuming as well.

15. The correct answer is: (A). In front of the school bus.

The front of the school bus is the safest place for students to cross the road after drop-off.

16. The correct answer is: (D). None of the above.

When checking around the vehicle for people or vehicles, check the crossover for approaching students, all the side mirrors and the crossover for exiting students. Checking everywhere is an effective way to reduce accidents that occur around school buses.

17. The correct answer is: (D). Both B and C.

After completing a route, don't simply switch off the engine and go home. Take a walk through the bus and check for sleeping students and forgotten articles. Check for acts of vandalism too. If you spot sleeping students, wake them up immediately. Return forgotten articles to the school.

18. The correct answer is: (A). Put the vehicle in neutral and engage the parking brake.

Before opening the door for loading and unloading, put the vehicle in neutral and engage the parking brake. This is important. It ensures that the vehicle remains stationary during the entire loading or unloading period. Thus, the vehicle can't roll over students or other road users.

19. The correct answer is: (D). Both A and C.

It is important that you are aware of your environment, especially what goes on in and around your vehicle. To enhance your hearing moving, silence the passengers. Don't forget to turn off noisy equipment that may interfere with your hearing.

20. The correct answer is: (D). All of the above.

Sometimes, accidents are caused by some simple things such as book bags, backpacks or jacket straps or strings being caught in the bus' doorway. Items tangled in the doorway can cause serious injuries.

21. The correct answer is: (C). At the beginning and throughout the school season.

The students' safety is one of your major responsibilities. At the beginning of the season, give them some practical safety tips. Throughout the school season, give them constant safety reminders.

22. The correct answer is: (B). Expose you and your passengers to risks.

When dropping off students, doing so at corners shortly before making a right turn is not ideal as it exposes both you and your passengers to needless risks. You have no idea what is happening around the corner. Perhaps there are incoming vehicles or other things that may expose you to risk.

23. The correct answer is: (B). Conduct a post-trip inspection.

After completing a trip, you should conduct a post-trip inspection. Close all open doors and windows. Check for operational or mechanical problems. Pay attention to the warning lights, mirror systems, stop signal arms, etc.

24. The correct answer is: (D). None of the above.

The post-trip inspection involves checking some major parts of the vehicle including warning lights, stop signal arms, etc.

25. The correct answer is: (B). Notify your supervisor or the school.

The inspection is to ensure that the vehicle is in good condition. If you notice problems, either notify your supervisor or the school authorities without delay. Let them rectify any issues you cannot address.

General Knowledge Test 2 – 50 Questions

1. If you are driving a 50-foot truck at 60 mph, how much space (in time) is needed between you and the next vehicle ahead of you?
    a. 4 seconds.
    b. 5 seconds.
    c. 6 seconds.
    d. 7 seconds.

2. You can take the road test on any day except:
    a. Wednesday.
    b. Saturday.
    c. Friday.
    d. Tuesday.

3. During a break while you are walking by your truck, you touch the tires of the truck and find them to be very hot. You should:
    a. Soak the tires with cool water and then begin driving the truck.
    b. Apply ice to the tires and then begin driving the truck.
    c. Wait until the tires are at normal temperature and then begin driving the truck.
    d. Begin driving the truck immediately, there is no need to wait.

4. While driving, you hear a tire burst on your truck. You should:
    a. Press the brakes so you can stop quickly.
    b. Press the brakes and also turn your truck to the side so other cars can pass.
    c. Do not press the brakes and hold the steering wheel without turning so that the truck comes to a stop by itself.
    d. Do not press the brakes and turn the steering wheel sharply so you can stop faster.

5. Engine braking occurs when:
    a. You change gears to a higher gear and press the brake.
    b. You change gears to a lower gear and press the brake.
    c. You change gears to a higher gear and take the foot off of the accelerator.
    d. You change gears to a lower gear and take the foot off of the accelerator.

6. If you fail the test on the first attempt, you can still retake the test a minimum of ... on a permit.
    a. Three times.
    b. Four times.
    c. Two times.
    d. Five times.

7. Your eligibility to apply for a permit will become invalid ...
    a. After two attempts.
    b. After five attempts.
    c. If you are physically unfit to operate a vehicle.
    d. None of the above.

8. If you are under 18 and fail the test, you must wait for ... before you can retake the examination.
    a. Seven days.
    b. Five days.
    c. As determined by the Department of Motor Vehicles.
    d. As determined by the local licensing and registration committee.

9. A Class 1 Truck is known as:
    a. A light truck and weighs between 0 and 6000 pounds.
    b. An ultra light truck and weighs between 0 and 6000 pounds.
    c. A medium truck and weighs between 0 and 6000 pounds.
    d. A light/medium truck and weighs between 0 and 6000 pounds.

10. Before you are allowed to reschedule your test, you must first ...
    a. Cancel your first appointment.
    b. Pay a rescheduling fee.
    c. Wait for three weeks after the first test.
    d. Wait for five weeks after the first test.

11. A Class 2a Truck is known as:
    a. Medium truck and weighs between 6000 pounds and 8,500 pounds.
    b. Light truck and weighs between 6,000 pounds and 8,500 pounds.
    c. Light/medium truck and weighs between 6,000 pounds and 8,500 pounds.
    d. Ultra light truck and weighs between 6,000 pounds and 8,500 pounds.

12. Under what conditions can you reschedule your test appointment?
    a. Change of job and inclement weather.
    b. Change of job.
    c. Inclement weather and tardiness to the exam center.
    d. Lack of interest in the exam and change of job.

13. You will fail the test if you do any of the following except:
    a. Run a red light.
    b. Cut corners driving on winding roads.
    c. Drive on curbs.
    d. None of the above.

14. While taking the test, a reckless driver nearly gets you involved in an accident. The best reaction is to ...
    a. Maintain your cool no matter what.
    b. Refuse to give the right of way.
    c. Respond aggressively.
    d. None of the above.

15. A Class 2b truck is known as:
    a. Medium truck and weighs between 8,500 pounds and 10,000 pounds.
    b. Light truck and weighs between 8,500 pounds and 10,000 pounds.
    c. Light/medium truck and weighs between 8,500 pounds and 10,000 pounds.
    d. Heavy truck and weighs between 8,500 pounds and 10,000 pounds.

16. To qualify for the road skills test, you must have a valid CLD for a minimum of ... before you schedule the test.
    a. 45 days.
    b. 30 days.
    c. 40 days.
    d. 60 days.

17. To take the road test, you should visit ...
    a. The nearest driving school.
    b. The Commercial Driver Road Test Lot.
    c. The Commercial Driver Road Test Park.
    d. The nearest licensing school.

18. When taking the road skills test, you should arrive at the test center ...
    a. 10 minutes early.
    b. 15 minutes early.
    c. 5 minutes early.
    d. 30 minutes early.

19. If you are under 21 and taking the road test, you must provide your ...
    a. 50-hour Certification of Eligibility for Provisional License form.
    b. 40-hour Certification of Eligibility for Provisional License form.
    c. 60-hour Certification of Eligibility for Provisional License form.
    d. 20-hour Certification of Eligibility for Provisional License form.

20. Each person taking the road skills test must be accompanied by ...
    a. A guarantor.
    b. A licensed driver.
    c. A driving school instructor.
    d. A lawyer.

21. If you drive yourself to the test center unaccompanied by the right person, you will be ...
    a. Banned from taking the test for 3 months.
    b. Banned from taking the test for 6 months.
    c. Banned from taking the test for 9 months.
    d. Banned from taking the test for 12 months.

22. A driver is required to devote a minimum of ... to practicing driving after sunset to prepare for night driving.
    a. 20 hours.
    b. 15 hours.
    c. 12 hours.
    d. 30 hours.

23. You should practice driving in both moderate and heavy traffic for ...
    a. 25 hours.
    b. 15 hours.
    c. 10 hours.
    d. 30 hours.

24. When should you stop the vehicle and bring it to a stop for the smoothest possible braking?
    a. As soon as you reach the stopping position.
    b. Shortly before reaching the stopping position.
    c. When it is convenient for you to do so.
    d. It depends on the type of vehicle you drive.

25. While shifting the gear, ... is an error you should avoid at all costs.
    a. Auto shifting.
    b. Grinding.
    c. Frictionless grinding.
    d. Abrupt shifting.

26. When approaching an intersection and asked to stop, where is the best position to stop the vehicle?
    a. Before the intersection.
    b. At the intersection.
    c. After the intersection.
    d. Wherever is convenient for you.

27. You should learn to stop your vehicle ...
    a. Before stop lines or crosswalks.
    b. At the stop lines or crosswalks.
    c. After the stop lines or crosswalks.
    d. At a convenient place.

28. Good driving habits include ...
    a. Identifying obstructions and avoiding them.
    b. Stopping your vehicle at a convenient location.
    c. Driving behind obstructions and hoping for the best.
    d. Driving as you feel comfortable.

29. Another good driving habit you should cultivate is ...
    a. Looking sideways only when driving.
    b. Observing your environment thoroughly.
    c. Depending exclusively on your mirrors for guidance.
    d. All of the above.

30. The benefits of paying attention to your environment include all of the following except:
    a. It makes it easier for you to spot potential problems.
    b. You can avoid obstacles that may impede your driving.
    c. It prevents you from colliding with other vehicles.
    d. None of the above.

31. When changing lanes, which of the following habits is a part of safe driving?
    a. Looking at your mirrors only.
    b. Looking over your shoulders only.
    c. Looking over your shoulders and your mirrors.
    d. Changing lanes whenever you need to.

32. Speed limits are usually posted beside roads and elsewhere for what purpose?
    a. To enable drivers to drive at a safe speed.
    b. To enable the authorities to show off their powers.
    c. They are not usually posted.
    d. None of the above.

33. Abiding by the speed limit ...
    a. Is proof of your safety consciousness.
    b. Shows you are incompetent at driving at faster speeds.
    c. Hampers your driving skills on highways.
    d. Slows your driving.

34. When driving in bad weather, what takes precedence?
    a. Speed limits take precedence over the bad weather.
    b. The bad weather takes precedence over speed limits.
    c. They take precedence over each other.
    d. They are both immaterial.

35. Besides bad weather, another reason for driving within the speed limit is ...
    a. The nature of the road.
    b. The type of vehicle you drive.
    c. The visibility.
    d. The condition of your tires.

36. Anticipating other drivers' actions ...
    a. Is only important for professional drivers.
    b. Is a test of your ability to deal with a wide range of drivers.
    c. Allows you to test how powerful your vehicle's horn is.
    d. Doesn't impact your driving.

37. What is the purpose of pavement markings?
    a. They convey important pieces of information to road users.
    b. They are designed to beautify roads.
    c. They indicate the beginning and end of a road.
    d. They have different meanings according to the prevailing circumstances.

38. Yellow lines on pavement serve what purpose?
    a. They serve as traffic separators.
    b. They serve as traffic warnings.
    c. They serve as security indicators.
    d. They serve as warnings about potential obstacles.

39. A solid yellow line means what?
    a. It indicates the part of the road designed for only cyclists.
    b. It indicates the part of the road closed to the public for an event.
    c. It indicates a part of the road undergoing renovation.
    d. It indicates parts of the road only meant for use in winter.

40. Yellow dashes mean what?
    a. The road is closed temporarily.
    b. The road is open for use.
    c. The road is for emergency use only.
    d. The road is under construction.

41. A minimum of ... points deducted is acceptable during a road skills test.
    a. 30.
    b. 20.
    c. 10.
    d. 50.

42. Getting involved in an accident during a road skills test will result in ...
    a. A $500 fine.
    b. Automatic disqualification.
    c. Automatic disqualification with a $200 fine.
    d. Automatic disqualification and a learner's permit revocation.

43. A B Class restriction on a driver's license indicates that ...
    a. The driver can only operate a vehicle with the assistance of corrective lenses.
    b. The driver is eligible to operate tankers.
    c. The driver can transport hazardous substances.
    d. The driver is limited to 18 passengers on their passenger bus.

44. A C Restriction on your license indicates that...
    a. You can only drive a vehicle with a mechanical aid.
    b. You can only drive a vehicle with a hearing aid.
    c. You can drive a wide range of commercial motor vehicles.
    d. None of the above.

45. An effective communication channel between drivers is the appropriate use of ...
    a. Indicators.
    b. Blinkers.
    c. Hand signals.
    d. Brake lights.

46. An E Restriction limits your driving to ...
    a. Commercial vehicles with an automatic transmission only.
    b. Commercial vehicles with a manual transmission only.
    c. Hybrid vehicles only.
    d. None of the above.

47. If you are restricted from night driving, you will be issued a license with a ...
    a. G Restriction.
    b. B Restriction.
    c. F Restriction.
    d. H Restriction.

48. The M Restriction restricts you from operating
    a. A Class A passenger vehicle or school bus under certain conditions.
    b. A Class B vehicle under certain conditions.
    c. A Class C vehicle under certain conditions.
    d. All classes of vehicle under certain conditions.

49. A general condition for overriding any of these restrictions is ...
    a. Holding a restriction-free Commercial Learner's Permit for 14 days.
    b. Holding a restriction-free Commercial Learner's Permit for 24 days.
    c. Holding a restriction-free Commercial Learner's Permit for 20 days.
    d. Holding a restriction-free Commercial Learner's Permit for 10 days.

50. If your driver's license carries an O Restriction, you can't operate ...
    a. Class A vehicles.
    b. Class B vehicles.
    c. Class C vehicles.
    d. Tractor trailer with a fifth-wheel connection.

General Knowledge Test 2 Answers

1. The correct answer is: (C). 6 seconds.

The general rule is that you need 1 second for each 10 feet of truck length while driving at 40 miles per hour. So if your speed is more than that, you need to add 1 additional second. Since the truck is 50-feet long, that means 5 seconds, plus 1 additional second. So the time is 6 seconds.

2. The correct answer is: (B). Saturday.

When planning your road test, you can only schedule an appointment on business days—Monday through Friday.

3. The correct answer is: (C). Wait until the tires are at normal temperature and then begin driving the truck.

It is recommended to wait until the tires are at normal temperature because it can be dangerous to drive on tires that are very hot.

4. The correct answer is: (C). Do not press the brakes and hold the steering wheel without turning so that the truck comes to a stop by itself.

You should not use the brake and you should not turn the steering wheel if the tire bursts. The safest way to stop is to remove the foot from the brakes and hold the steering wheel firmly.

5. The correct answer is: (D). You change gears to a lower gear and take the foot off of the accelerator.

This technique is recommended for slowing down the vehicle when moving too fast on a steep declining road.

6. The correct answer is: (C). Two times.

If you fail the test on the first attempt, you can still take the exam two times on your permit. The rule allows each permit holder to take the exam a maximum of three times. This is to enable drivers to prepare in advance for the test.

7. The correct answer is: (C). If you are physically unfit to operate a vehicle.

If you exhaust the three chances allocated to a driver on a learner's permit, you can apply for another permit and have three more chances to attempt the test. However, your permission to apply for the license becomes null and void if you are physically unfit to operate a vehicle.

8. The correct answer is: (A). Seven days.

If you are under 28 and fail the test, you must allow a seven-day interval before reapplying to take the exam.

9. The correct answer is: (B). Go through your study materials again and improve your driving skills.

While waiting to submit your retake application, keep studying and practicing your driving. Make good use of your time in between tests.

10. The correct answer is: (A). Cancel your first appointment.

Before you are allowed to reschedule your driver's license test, it is mandatory that you cancel your first appointment.

11. The correct answer is: (B). Light truck and weighs between 6,000 pounds and 8,500 pounds.

Class 2a is made up of light trucks.

12. The correct answer is: (A). Change of job and inclement weather.

There are several reasons why you may consider rescheduling your test appointment. Some of these reasons included a change of job and inclement weather. If you are late to the examination center, that's your fault. It is not a genuine reason for changing your test date.

13. The correct answer is: (D). None of the above.

Running a red light, driving on curbs and cutting corners when driving on winding roads are some of the bad driving habits that may cost you your license. If you engage in any of these habits while taking the test, your examiner will score you low.

14. The correct answer is: (A). Maintain your cool no matter what.

During the test, you will have to contend with different challenges such as reckless drivers who don't care about other road users. When another driver nearly gets you involved in an accident, don't lose your cool. Your reaction will tell an examiner a lot about you.

15. The correct answer is: (C). Light/medium truck and weighs between 8,500 pounds and 10,000 pounds.

Light/medium trucks make up Class 2b.

16. The correct answer is: (B). 30 days.

To qualify for the road skills test, you must have a valid CDL for a minimum of 30 days before scheduling the test.

17. The correct answer is: (B). The Commercial Driver Road Test Lot.

As a prerequisite for obtaining the license, visit the Commercial Driver Road Test Lot.

18. The correct answer is: (B). 15 minutes.

When taking any test, including the road skills test, make sure you always arrive at least 15 minutes early to the testing center.

19. The correct answer is: (B). 40-hour Certification of Eligibility for Provisional License form.

If you are under 21 and taking the road test, you must provide proof of your driving ability and skills. This includes a 40-hour Certification of Eligibility for Provisional License form.

20. The correct answer is: (b). A licensed driver.

Each license applicant taking the test is expected to be accompanied by a licensed driver, especially if you drive yourself to the center. This is to ensure that you have someone to guide you as you drive to the test center and back home.

21. The correct answer is: (B). Banned from taking the test for six months.

If you drive yourself to the test center without a licensed driver to guide you, you stand the risk of being banned from taking the test for six months.

22. The correct answer is: (B). 15 hours.

While honing your driving skills, you are expected to learn how to drive a commercial vehicle of your choice under different conditions. This includes learning how to drive at night.

23. The correct answer is: (C). 10 hours.

Your driving practice should cover areas of moderate to heavy traffic as well. You are required to dedicate at least 10 hours to driving under such conditions. The more you practice, the better you become.

24. The correct answer is: (B). Shortly before reaching the stopping position.

You should avoid jerky braking. To do this, stop the vehicle and bring it to a rest shortly before reaching the stopping position.

25. The correct answer is: (B). Grinding.

Grinding is a common error among new and inexperienced drivers. To pass the test, you must avoid committing this error at all costs.

26. The correct answer is: (A). Before the intersection.

When you are approaching an intersection and your examiner asks you to stop, you must stop the vehicle before the intersection. This enables you to have a clear view of the intersection whenever you pull out.

27. The correct answer is: (A). Before stop lines or crosswalks.

When approaching crosswalks or stop lines, stopping before them is a good driving habit for safety's sake.

28. The correct answer is: (A). Identifying obstructions and avoiding them.

Good driving habits ensure your safety on the road. They guarantee the safety of other road users as well. Hence, endeavor to identify obstructions when driving. As much as possible, avoid them at all costs. Don't deliberately put yourself in situations that make driving more difficult for you.

29. The correct answer is: (B). Observing your environment thoroughly.

The road ahead shouldn't be your only concern when you are behind the wheel. Take your environment into consideration too. Look sideways when driving to spot potential problems and avoid them. Check your mirrors regularly as well. You can't ever be too careful. Do whatever it takes to be safe.

30. The correct answer is: (D). None of the above.

You benefit a lot if you pay attention to your environment when you are behind the wheel. Aside from making it easier for you to identify potential problems and avoid them, it also enables you to drive with ease. Your chances of running into other vehicles are reduced too.

31. The correct answer is: (C). Looking over your shoulders and your mirrors.

When you wish to change lanes, don't assume that other road users are aware of your intentions. That may land you in trouble. Rather, look over your shoulders to check the vehicles behind you. Check your mirrors for oncoming vehicles from other sides too.

32. The correct answer is: (A). To enable drivers to drive at a safe speed.

When driving, you may see speed limits posted. They serve as reminders to drive at a safe speed for your sake and that of others.

33. The correct answer is: (A). It's proof of your safety consciousness.

Abiding by the speed limits is proof of your safety consciousness. If you violate them, you are invariably showing your lack of respect for your safety and the safety of others.

34. The correct answer is: (B). The bad weather takes precedence over speed limits.

When driving in bad weather, you are not obligated to keep to the speed limit. The bad weather takes precedence. The rule of thumb is to drive at a speed that ensures everyone's safety.

35. The correct answer is: (C). The visibility.

Besides bad weather, another factor you should consider when considering whether to drive at the exact posted speed limit is visibility. Hitting 60 miles/hour if you can barely see is a bad idea. It may be safer to keep to 20 miles/hour until the weather clears.

36. The correct answer is: (B). A test of your ability to deal with a wide range of drivers.

While driving, it is dangerous to focus only on your own driving. You must consider other road users as well. Their driving decisions may affect you. Hence, anticipate their actions and make adequate preparations for them.

37. The correct answer is: (A). Markings that convey important pieces of information to road users.

Pavement markings are used to convey important messages to road users. Abiding by that information helps keep everyone on the road safe.

38. The correct answer is: (A). They serve as traffic separators.

Yellow lines serve as traffic separators so that vehicles going in opposite directions won't run into each other.

39. The correct answer is: (B). It indicates the part of the road closed to the public.

A solid yellow pavement marking indicates the part of the road closed to the public for a particular reason such as repairs being made.

40. The correct answer is: (B). The road is open for use.

While yellow dashes indicate you should steer clear, yellow markings mean the opposite. They indicate that part of the road is safe to use.

41. The correct answer is: (A). 30.

For each driving rule you violate during the road skills test, your examiner will deduct points. The acceptable limit is 30. A driver who has more than 30 points deducted during the test has failed. This underscores the importance of obeying every driving rule while taking the test.

42. The correct answer is: (B). Automatic disqualification.

If you get involved in an accident while taking the road skills test, you have automatically failed the exam.

43. The correct answer is: (A). The driver can only operate a vehicle with the assistance of corrective lenses.

If you have a B restriction on your driver's license, this implies that you are only licensed to operate a vehicle with the assistance of corrective lenses. Hence, if you must use corrective lenses, you will not be allowed to operate the vehicle without wearing them.

44. The correct answer is: (A). You can only drive a vehicle with a mechanical aid.

A C Restriction on your license indicates that you are only permitted to drive a vehicle with a mechanical aid. Failure to do so will result in consequences.

45. The correct answer is: (B). Blinkers.

An effective communication channel between drivers is the effective use of blinkers. They signal to drivers where you are planning to turn so that they can then stay out of the way and remain safe.

46. The correct answer is: (A). Commercial vehicles with an automatic transmission only.

You can only drive commercial vehicles with an automatic transmission if you have an E Restriction. Thus, if you wish to operate commercial vehicles with manual transmission systems, this restriction does not allow for that.

47. The correct answer is: (A). G Restriction.

Not every driver can handle night driving. Individuals who cannot see well at night or who simply don't drive well at night, for whatever reason, are issued a license with a G Restriction.

48. The correct answer is: (A). A Class A passenger vehicle or school bus under certain conditions.

An M Restriction is another form of restriction for drivers who drive school bus or class A passenger vehicles. Such drivers are prevented from operating school buses or passenger vehicles if the skills test for this special endorsement was done with a class B passenger vehicle.

49. The correct answer is: (A). Holding a restriction-free Commercial Learner's Permit for 14 days.

A general condition for overriding any of these restrictions is to hold a restriction-free Commercial Learner's Permit for 14 days. At that point, the license will be replaced with a license without the restriction, provided that you satisfy other conditions.

50. The correct answer is: (D). Tractor trailer with a fifth-wheel connection

The O restriction forbids drivers from operating commercial motor vehicle tractors of any sort. Thus, if this appears on your commercial learner's permit or driver's license, a tractor with a fifth-wheel connection is off the list of vehicles you can operate.

Air Brakes Test 2 – 25 Questions

1. What happens when a vehicle equipped with air brakes is idle?
    a. The vehicle will lose its air pressure.
    b. The contaminants can settle easily.
    c. The vehicle's air system will be charged.
    d. Nothing will happen to the vehicle.

2. What effect does depressing the brake pedal have on the pressure?
    a. The pressure remains stationary.
    b. The pressure increases gradually.
    c. The pressure decreases gradually.
    d. The pressure evaporates gradually.

3. Which parts of the air brakes support the compressor?
    a. The emergency air brakes.
    b. The compressor governor.
    c. The air tank drains.
    d. None of the above.

4. What must you do before driving a vehicle equipped with the air brake system?
    a. Empty the air drain tank.
    b. Push the emergency brake.
    c. Depress the brakes.
    d. Test the horns and the blinkers.

5. What produces the force applied to a vehicle's wheels for effective braking?
    a. Compressed air.
    b. Mechanical force produced by the brake system.
    c. The brake pedal.
    d. The air tank governor.

6. What occurs when the brake pedal is pressed?
    a. The compressed air is released.
    b. The compressed air is compressed further.
    c. The compressed air is circulated through the braking system.
    d. The compressed air becomes hot.

7. The air brake system is a combination of ...
    a. Four braking systems.
    b. Five braking systems.
    c. Two braking systems.
    d. Three braking systems.

8. This braking system applies and releases the brakes when you apply the brakes while driving normally.
    a. The Parking Brake System.
    b. The Service Brake System.
    c. The Control Brake System.
    d. The Automatic Brake System.

9. To use the ... its air must be routed under pressure at approximately 100 to 120 psi.
    a. Parking Brake System.
    b. Service Brake System.
    c. Control Brake System.
    d. Automatic Brake System.

10. This brake is otherwise known as a hand brake or e-brake ...
    a. The Service Brake System.
    b. The Parking Brake System.
    c. The Emergency Brake System.
    d. The Automatic Brake System.

11. How do heavy vehicle drivers know whether there is enough pressure in the brake system or not?
    a. Through the air pressure meter.
    b. Through a built-in gauge.
    c. Through an air pressure compressor governor.
    d. None of the above.

12. What is a wig wag?
    a. A device that indicates when the brake is faulty.
    b. A device that indicates that the air pressure is below the recommended level.
    c. A device for measuring brake efficiency.
    d. A device for fixing faulty brakes.

13. The air pressure warning signal goes off when ...
    a. The pressure in the air pressure tank is below 60 psi.
    b. When the pressure in the tank is below 50 psi.
    c. When the pressure in the tank is below 100 psi.
    d. When the pressure in the tank is below 45 psi

14. Under what conditions can the warning signal go off when the pressure is between 80 and 85 psi?
    a. When driving a large bus.
    b. When driving a trailer tractor.
    c. When driving a passenger bus.
    d. When driving a tanker.

15. The compressed air brake system is classified into ...
    a. Three classes.
    b. Four classes.
    c. Two classes.
    d. Five classes.

16. Two service brake circuits, a parking brake circuit and a trailer brake circuit are some components of the ...
    a. Circuit system.
    b. Brake system.
    c. Supply system.
    d. Control system.

17. A brake pedal air valve regulates the ... and ...
    a. Front and rear wheel circuits.
    b. Parking brake and trailer brake circuits.
    c. Parking and wheel circuits.
    d. Front and trailer brake circuits.

18. Which of these components does the engine use to drive the air compressor?
    a. A crankshaft pulley or a belt.
    b. A crankshaft pulley or an iron chain.
    c. An iron chain or a crankshaft pulley.
    d. None of the above.

19. What must you do first to test your low pressure warning signal?
    a. Apply the brake first.
    b. Turn off the engine.
    c. Check the air compressor.
    d. Reduce the pressure in the air tank.

20. Under what conditions should you test your vehicle's air leakage rate?
    a. When the system is half charged.
    b. When the air pressure is between 200 and 250 psi.
    c. When the system is fully charged.
    d. When the vehicle's engine has been run continuously for five hours.

21. The recommended operating pressure per square inch for a bus' brake system is ...
    a. 60 pounds per square inch.
    b. 80 pounds per square inch.
    c. 85 pounds per square inch.
    d. 50 pounds per square inch.

22. A reasonable air leakage rate for combination vehicles is ...
    a. No more than 8 psi.
    b. More than 5 psi.
    c. No more than 4 psi.
    d. 10 psi.

23. Under what conditions should you be concerned about the cracks in the brake drums or discs?
    a. If the cracks are less than one inch long.
    b. If the cracks are shorter than half the width of the areas allowed for friction.
    c. If the cracks are longer than half the width of the areas allowed for friction.
    d. It depends on the type of vehicle.

24. When driving a vehicle equipped with a dual air brake system, you should always ...
    a. Allow sufficient time for the air pressure in the air compressor to build up.
    b. Allow sufficient time for the air pressure in the air compressor to be reduced drastically.
    c. Allow sufficient time for the air pressure in the air compressor to rise somewhat.
    d. Do nothing.

25. The dual air brake is divided into the ... and ...
    a. Front and rear system.
    b. Primary and secondary systems.
    c. Manual and automatic system.
    d. Stop and start system.

Air Brake Test 2 Answers

1. The correct answer is: (C). The vehicle's air system will be charged.

When a vehicle equipped with air brakes is parked, the vehicle's air system will be charged as the brake is not depressed. Then, the air pressure in the brake system will overcome the S-Cam or the diaphragm in a closed position. This will result in the brake system being released.

2. The correct answer is: (C). The pressure decreases gradually.

If you depress the brake, the pressure will decrease gradually. The decrease will turn the S-Cam while the brake shoes are simultaneously spread against the drum. This will cause the reservoir tanks to be filled by the compressor so that the air pressure increases again as the pedal retracts.

3. The correct answer is: (A). The emergency air brakes.

The emergency air brakes support the compressor. They work to enhance the performance of the air brake system by enabling drivers to stop their vehicles during emergencies. You can activate the system by pulling the emergency air brake button on the dash.

4. The correct answer is: (B). Push the emergency brake.

Before you drive a vehicle equipped with the air brake system, push its emergency brake in. That will give the air brake system enough air before you drive the vehicle. The emergency brake will remain in a free state once the emergency system is pressurized.

5. The correct answer is: (B). Mechanical force produced by the brake system.

The mechanical force produced by the brake system produces the force applied to a vehicle's wheels for effective braking. The mechanical force prevents accidental leakage of the air pressure that the vehicle needs for braking. Thus, the vehicle's brakes have what they need to function properly.

6. The correct answer is: (C). The compressed air is circulated through the braking system.

When the brake pedal is pressed, the compressed air in the system is circulated from one part of the braking system to another part. This makes braking possible as the entire system has air to function.

7. The correct answer is: (D). Three braking systems.

The air brake system is made up of three braking systems. These are the Service Brake System, the Parking Brake System and the Emergency Brake System. The combination of these components enables the driver to use the appropriate system to stop the vehicle under different conditions.

8. The correct answer is: (B). The Service Brake System.

The Service Brake System applies and releases the brakes when you apply the brakes under normal driving conditions. It is used for slow driving or stopping rather than for emergencies when the brake doesn't function properly.

9. The correct answer is: (B). The Service Brake System.

You can only use the Service Brake System by routing its air under pressure at approximately 100 to 120 psi to the vehicle's brake chamber. This will engage the brake and make the vehicle stop or slow down, as needed.

10. The correct answer is: (C). The Emergency Brake System.

The Emergency Brake System is otherwise known as an e-brake or hand brake. It is a braking system that allows you to stop your vehicle whenever you want and prevent unfortunate accidents. Aside from its use during emergencies, it can also be used to keep vehicles motionless when parked.

11. The correct answer is: (B). Through a built-in gauge.

Modern heavy vehicles are designed with a built-in gauge that monitors the air pressure in the brake. You may get a warning light or hear a sound if the air pressure is way below the recommended level. This enables you to know whether the system is faulty or working properly.

12. The correct answer is: (B). A device that indicates the air pressure is below the recommended level.

A wig wag is a device that drops down automatically to indicate the air pressure is below the recommended level. This enables the driver to see the low level and act promptly.

13. The correct answer is: (A). The pressure in the air pressure tank is below 60 psi.

If the pressure in the air pressure tank goes below 60 psi, the warning signal will go off. The warning indicates that the vehicle is not safe to drive at the moment.

14. The correct answer is: (A). When driving a large bus.

The air pressure warning signal goes off when the pressure in the tank goes below 60 psi. However, there is an exception. When driving a large bus, the signal will only go off when the pressure is between 80 and 85 psi.

15. The correct answer is: (C). Two classes.

The compressed air brake system is classified into the Control System and the Supply System. The former controls all the activities in the brake system while the latter comprises different checks, safety valves and a drain valve. It supplies everything the brake needs.

16. The correct answer is: (D). Control System.

Two service brakes, a parking brake circuit and a trailer brake circuit are some components of the Control System. It uses these components to control all the activities that go on in the brake system.

17. The correct answer is: (A). Front and rear wheel circuits.

A brake pedal air valve regulates the front and rear wheel circuits. These circuits receive compressed air from the different reservoirs to serve as a source of added safety for the vehicle, especially if there is an air leak. It helps to minimize the impact of any such leak.

18. The correct answer is: (A). A crankshaft pulley or a belt.

The vehicle's engine uses a crankshaft pulley or a belt to drive the air compressor. Vehicles use fuel to generate power. The power is distributed to different components of the vehicle through the mechanical and electrical systems. A crankshaft pulley is a major component for power distribution.

19. The correct answer is: (B). Turn off the engine.

The first step for a low pressure warning signal test is to turn off the engine. Then, make sure that the air pressure is enough so that the low pressure warning signal isn't already activated before you start the test. Then, turn the electrical power on to proceed.

20. The correct answer is: (C). When the system is fully charged.

You should only test the air leakage rate when the system is fully charged. That is about 125 psi. Release the parking brake after turning off the engine. Time the rate at which the air pressure drops. If the loss rate is more than 2 psi/minute for single vehicles, that's a problem.

21. The correct answer is: (C). 85 pounds psi.

The recommended operating pressure per square inch for a bus' brake system is 85. At that pressure, the brake system will function at optimal capacity and reduce the risk of brake failure and other related issues.

22. The correct answer is: (C). No more than 4 psi.

For combination vehicles, the reasonable air leakage rate mustn't be more than 4 psi. Otherwise, the leakage rate is too much and can damage the vehicle.

23. The correct answer is: (C). If the cracks are longer than half the width of the area allowed for friction.

Brake drums or discs have cracks by default. However, you should be concerned about these cracks if they are longer than half the width of the areas allowed for friction. The longer cracks may interfere with the operations of the drums or discs and undermine the brake system's efficiency.

24. The correct answer is: (A). Allow sufficient time for the air pressure in the air compressor to build up significantly.

When driving a vehicle that is equipped with a dual air brake system, allow sufficient time for the air pressure in the compressor to build up significantly to 100 psi or more in both the secondary and primary systems.

25. The correct answer is: (B). The dual air brake is divided into primary and secondary systems.

The dual air brake system is divided into primary and secondary systems. The primary system controls the brakes at the rear axles while the secondary system takes care of the front axle, and sometimes, a rear axle. Both of these systems serve as air suppliers to the trailer.

Hazmat Test 2 – 25 Questions

1. All of the following are endorsement requirements for transporting hazardous materials except:
    a. A valid CDL permit.
    b. Proof of identity.
    c. A valid certificate from a medical examiner.
    d. Proof of residency.

2. Which of these is acceptable proof of identity for a US citizen?
    a. Certificate of US Citizenship.
    b. A US passport.
    c. Certificate of naturalization.
    d. All of the above.

3. There are ... classes of hazmat endorsement.
    a. Two.
    b. Five.
    c. Four.
    d. Three.

4. This hazmat endorsement type is required for driving tankers ...
    a. P Endorsement.
    b. K Endorsement.
    c. N Endorsement.
    d. X Endorsement.

5. This is considered the ultimate endorsement class ...
    a. X Endorsement.
    b. H Endorsement.
    c. V Endorsement.
    d. Y Endorsement.

6. A hazmat endorsement on your Commercial Driver's License will cost you ...
    a. $100.
    b. $150.
    c. $50.
    d. $200.

7. You can get a discount if you are ...
    a. A new applicant with a Commercial Learner's Permit.
    b. A new applicant with a valid TWIC card.
    c. A new applicant with five years' driving experience.
    d. A new applicant without a criminal record.

8. What is a TWIC?
    a. Transport Worker Identification Card.
    b. Transport Worker Identification Column Card.
    c. Transportation Worker Identification Credential.
    d. None of the above.

9. A hazmat endorsement is valid for ...
    a. Ten years.
    b. Fifteen years.
    c. Five years.
    d. Four years.

10. Which of the following information is not required on a TSA application?
    a. Middle name.
    b. Date of birth.
    c. Preferred method of contact.
    d. None of the above.

11. The most important pieces of information on the TSA application are:
    a. Phone number and email address.
    b. Name and contact method.
    c. Date of birth and zip code.
    d. Gender and middle name.

12. Which of the following is/are not allowed in the name fields on the application form?
    a. Apostrophe.
    b. Hyphens.
    c. Letters.
    d. Special characters.

13. Do you have to take the assessment in a certain place?
    a. Yes.
    b. It depends on the examiner.
    c. No.
    d. It depends on you.

14. You need all of the following information to choose a location except:
    a. The test you want to take.
    b. Your zip code.
    c. Your city.
    d. Your credit history.

15. The passing grade for the hazmat endorsement test is ...
    a. 74%.
    b. 85%.
    c. 90%.
    d. 80%.

16. You are allowed to retake the exam ...
    a. As many times as possible.
    b. 8 times.
    c. Less than 5 times.
    d. Up to 10 times.

17. Is retaking the test free?
    a. Yes.
    b. No.
    c. It is free for the first two times but you must pay for subsequent retakes.
    d. You must pay for the first two retakes while subsequent ones are free.

18. The assessment test will assess your knowledge of all of the following except:
    a. Your ability to identify hazardous materials.
    b. Your ability to placard your vehicle according to established rules.
    c. Your ability to load shipments safely.
    d. None of the above.

19. The vessels that an applicant with TWIC card has access to are regulated by the ...
    a. Maritime Transportation Security Act of 2010.
    b. Maritime Transportation Security Act of 2000.
    c. Maritime Transportation Security Act of 2015.
    d. Maritime Transportation Security Act of 2002.

20. What makes up the cost of a hazmat endorsement?
    a. TSA charges plus state charges.
    b. State charges plus federal charges.
    c. TSA charges plus federal charges.
    d. TSA, state and federal charges.

21. Drivers who transport placarded hazardous materials need a ...
    a. C Endorsement.
    b. P Endorsement.
    c. M Endorsement.
    d. H Endorsement.

22. The DOT Card is otherwise known as a ...
    a. Medical History Certificate.
    b. Medical Health Record.
    c. Medical Examiner's Credentials.
    d. Medical Examiner's Certificate.

23. Hazmat endorsements are classified into ...
    a. H Endorsement, P Endorsement and K Endorsement.
    b. P Endorsement, Y Endorsement and V Endorsement.
    c. H Endorsement, X Endorsement and N Endorsement.
    d. V Endorsement, F Endorsement and E Endorsement.

24. If your waiver or appeal is granted, you and the ... will be notified.
    a. State government.
    b. Federal government.
    c. Local Department of Motor Vehicles.
    d. All of the above.

25. All of the following are ways to identify hazardous materials except ...
    a. A highlighted entry.
    b. An X or H endorsement.
    c. Placarding.
    d. None of the above.

Hazmat Test 2 Answers

1. The correct answer is: (D). Proof of residency.

To transport hazardous materials, you need a valid CDL permit, a valid certificate from a medical examiner and proof of identity.

2. The correct answer is: (D). All of the above.

To prove your identity when applying for the endorsement, the testing center will accept your US passport, certificate of birth issued by a government-approved body, certificate of naturalization or certificate of US Citizenship. If you can't provide any of these, your identity can't be confirmed and your endorsement application will be rejected.

3. The correct answer is: (D). Three classes.

There are three classes of hazmat endorsement. These are the H Endorsement, X Endorsement and N Endorsement. Each endorsement allows you to drive under certain conditions.

4. The correct answer is: (C). N Endorsement.

If you wish to transport hazardous materials in a tanker, you need the N Endorsement on your CDL. The tank must be either temporarily or permanently attached to the chassis or the vehicle. Passing the Tank Knowledge Test is a requirement for getting this endorsement.

5. The correct answer is: (A). X Endorsement.

The X Endorsement is considered the ultimate endorsement class because with it, you can handle tanks and other hazardous materials. However, before you can obtain the X endorsement on your CDL, you must pass a test for hazardous materials as well as a skills and knowledge test for tankers.

6. The correct answer is: (A). $100.

The total cost of the hazmat endorsement on a driver's license is $100. The TSA charges $86.50 for screening and some others fees charged by the state bring the grand total to $100. None of these fees can be waived.

7. The correct answer is: (B). A new applicant with a valid TWIC card.

If you are a new applicant with a valid Transportation Worker Identification Credential card, you can enjoy the new reduced rate for such applicants: $67.

8. The correct answer is: (C). Transportation Worker Identification Credential.

A Transportation Worker Identification Credential (TWIC) gives the holder access to outer continental shelf facilities and port facilities that are regulated by the Maritime Transportation Security Act of 2002 with the primary objective of addressing port security across the country.

9. The correct answer is: (C). Five years.

If you are granted a hazmat endorsement after meeting all the requirements, the endorsement has a validity period of five years.

10. The correct answer is: (D). None of the above.

The TSA application requires your middle name, first name, date of birth, phone number and email address.

11. The correct answer is: (A). Phone number and email address.

Although you are required to provide a long list of useful pieces of information, phone number and email address are most important so that you can be contacted as needed.

12. The correct answer is: (D). Special characters.

The name field allows for letters, apostrophe, hyphens and spaces. However, special characters are not allowed. Failure to abide by this rule may invalidate your application.

13. The correct answer is: (C). No.

Applicants are not restricted to a specific location to take the test so long as it is within an applicant's state of residence. Visit the TSA's website and use the Enrollment Center Locator to choose where you take the assessment.

14. The correct answer is: (D). Your credit history.

To choose a convenient location, you must provide the following information: your zip code, city, the test you wish to enroll for and other pieces of relevant information. Your credit history will not be required.

15. The correct answer is: (D). 80%.

80% is the passing grade for the test. The section contains 30 questions and you are required to score a minimum of 24/30 to meet that percentage.

16. The correct answer is: (A). As many times as possible.

If you fail the test, you can take it as many times as necessary to pass it,

17. The correct answer is: (B). No.

You must pay all the necessary fees before being allowed to retake the test. However, you must wait for at least three days after the first test before submitting an application for a retake.

18. The correct answer is: (D). None of the above.

While taking the assessment, your knowledge in several areas will be tested. This includes your ability to identify hazardous materials, load shipments safely and placard your vehicle according to established rules.

19. The correct answer is: (D). Maritime Transportation Security Act of 2002.

A TWIC card grants its holders access to some vessels. These vessels are regulated by the Maritime Transportation Security Act of 2002. Among other things, the act was enacted by the US Congress to ensure safer roads for all users.

20. The correct answer is: (A). TSA charges plus state charges.

When applying for a hazmat endorsement, you are required to pay fees including TSA charges and state charges, totaling $100.

21. The correct answer is: (D). H Endorsement.

Drivers who transport placarded hazardous materials need an H Endorsement. It is imperative that you are familiar with both state and federal laws that guide the transportation of placarded hazardous materials and abide by them.

22. The correct answer is: (D). Medical Examiner's Certificate.

The DOT Card is otherwise known as the Medical Examiner's Certificate. This card is issued to drivers who pass the physical exam showing that they are physically fit to handle commercial vehicles for transporting hazardous materials. The medical certification process is overseen by the Federal Motor Carrier Safety Administration.

23. The correct answer is: (C). H Endorsement, X Endorsement and N Endorsement.

Hazardous endorsements are classified into the H Endorsement, X Endorsement and N Endorsement. An H Endorsement permits you to transport placarded hazardous materials while N and X Endorsements provide different permissions.

24. The correct answer is: (A). State government.

If the TSA grants your appeal or waiver, it will inform both you and the state government. This is to enable the state to be fully aware of your current status as well as the cancellation of your disqualification. Thus, you can then get the right endorsement, depending on your needs.

25. The correct answer is: (D). None of the above.

If a hazardous material contains an entry with an RQ or X in the appropriate column, you are handling a harmful material. A highlighted entry also indicates dangerous chemicals or materials. If you see any of these, you are transporting hazardous materials.

Doubles and Triples Test 2 – 25 Questions

1. How do you prevent the rig from moving?
    a. By using the emergency brakes.
    b. By using the parking brakes.
    c. By using both the emergency and parking brakes.
    d. All of the above.

2. When uncoupling the converter dolly, what comes first?
    a. Lowering the landing gear.
    b. Connecting safety chains.
    c. Releasing the pintle hook.
    d. Moving away from the dolly slowly.

3. When is it unwise to detach or unlock the pintle hook?
    a. After lowering the landing gear.
    b. Before chocking the wheels.
    c. After releasing the pintle hook.
    d. When the dolly is under the rear trailer.

4. When coupling a triple trailer, which of these parts must be coupled first?
    a. The first and second trailers.
    b. The third and fourth trailers.
    c. The second and third trailers.
    d. It depends on the type of vehicle.

5. The first thing you must do when uncoupling a triple trailer is ...
    a. Uncouple the second and third trailer first.
    b. Uncouple the first and second trailer.
    c. Pull the dolly out and unhitch it.
    d. Unhitch the third trailer first.

6. During an inspection, which part of the double or triple trailer must you check first?
    a. The lubrication.
    b. The locking jaws.
    c. The lower section of the wheel.
    d. The upper fifth wheel.

7. Spaces between the lower and upper fifth wheel are a sign of what problem?
    a. The fifth wheel is not properly connected.
    b. A bolt has worn out.
    c. It is not properly lubricated.
    d. A part is missing.

8. What should you do when in doubt about the best way to couple or uncouple a trailer?
    a. Use your discretion.
    b. Check the manufacturer's handbook.
    c. All of the above.
    d. None of the above.

9. When you are checking the lower part of the fifth wheel, you should focus on all of the following except:
    a. The lubrication.
    b. The locking jaws.
    c. The release arm.
    d. None of the above.

10. The glide plate should be mounted ...
    a. On the trailer rear.
    b. On the trailer frame.
    c. On the fifth wheel.
    d. Beside the kingpin.

11. While is it important to check the distance between the fifth wheel and the tractor frame?
    a. To ensure they avoid hitting each other during turns.
    b. To ensure the connection is solid.
    c. To ensure that nothing can get between them and interfere with their operations.
    d. It's a preventive measure against disconnecting when the vehicle is in motion.

12. For the best performance, the landing gear must be ...
    a. Reasonably raised.
    b. Partially raised.
    c. Fully raised.
    d. Not raised.

13. The tractor air supply control is otherwise known as a ...
    a. Trailer emergency valve.
    b. Tractor protection valve control.
    c. Tractor emergency valve control.
    d. Both A and B.

14. Check all of the following in the trailer emergency brakes except the:
    a. Emergency position.
    b. Air pressure.
    c. Brake parts.
    d. None of the above.

15. When testing airflow to the trailer, it is important that you first ...
    a. Chock the wheels or apply the brakes.
    b. Wait until the air pressure is normal.
    c. Push the trailer air supply knob.
    d. Use an air pressure meter to read the current air pressure.

16. The last step when testing airflow to the trailer is ...
    a. Supplying air to the service line.
    b. Pushing the trailer air supply knob.
    c. Waiting until the air pressure normalizes.
    d. Reading the air pressure with a meter.

17. This type of brake is needed for intermittent testing:
    a. An emergency brake system.
    b. A trailer service brake.
    c. A hand brake.
    d. An e-brake.

18. All of the following parts of a trailer service brake need to be thoroughly checked except:
    a. The air pressure.
    b. The air pressure meter.
    c. The brake's reliability.
    d. Both A and C.

19. You can protect the tractor air brake system with the ...
    a. Air brake protector.
    b. Trailer brake guard.
    c. Tractor protection valve.
    d. Automated parking brake protector.

20. At what air pressure range should you stop airflow to the trailer?
    a. 40 to 50 psi.
    b. 50 to 60 psi.
    c. 20 to 45 psi.
    d. 33 to 40 psi.

21. When checking the power-operated landing gear, you should always make sure to check ...
    a. The power button.
    b. The landing gear and power connector.
    c. Air leaks.
    d. Landing gear protector.

22. How do you remove some of the weight on a dolly?
    a. By offloading the vehicle.
    b. By removing the landing gear.
    c. By lowering the second trailer's landing gear.
    d. By detaching the second trailer.

23. How do you check the second trailer for air?
    a. Through the emergency line shutoff.
    b. Through the air meter.
    c. By lifting the valve over it.
    d. By increasing the air pressure level.

24. The crack-the-whip effect occurs mostly in the ... of a combination vehicle.
    a. The tractor.
    b. The connecting section.
    c. The trailer.
    d. A and C.

25. As a double or triple trailer driver, are you allowed to operate in all US states?
    a. Yes.
    b. The DMV must decide. .
    c. It depends on the years of experience and the driver's age.
    d. No.

Doubles and Triples Test 2 Answers

1. The correct answer is: (B). By using the parking brakes.

The parking brakes are designed to stop a vehicle from moving. When working on a double or triple trailer, apply the hand brake to keep the vehicle stationary until you are ready to move it. Alternatively, if the brake is faulty, chock the wheels to ensure the vehicle doesn't move.

2. The correct answer is: (A). Lowering the landing gear.

When uncoupling the converter dolly, the first step is to lower the landing gear. Then, disconnect the safety pins. This will give you access to other parts of the converter dolly you need to inspect.

3. The correct answer is: (D). When the dolly is under the rear trailer.

A good safety precaution when handling a double or triple trailer is to never detach or unlock the pintle hook when the dolly is under the rear trailer. If you unlock it in that condition, the trailer's weight makes the right hitch fly up and this can cause damage.

4. The correct answer is: (A). The first and second trailers.

The first and second trailers must be connected first when coupling a triple trailer.

5. The correct answer is: (C). Pull the dolly out and unhitch it.

When you are uncoupling your triple trailer, pull the dolly out first and unhitch it. After unhitching the dolly, you gain unrestricted access to the other parts of the vehicle on your checklist.

6. The correct answer is: (C). The lower section of the wheel.

The lower section of the fifth wheel should be checked first. The locking jaws and release arm are some of the areas you should inspect for possible damage or missing parts.

7. The correct answer is: (C). It is not properly lubricated.

The lower and upper sections of the fifth wheel are supposed to be close. If there are spaces between them, that's an indicator that the fifth wheel is not properly lubricated.

8. The correct answer is: (B). Check the manufacturer's handbook.

Sometimes, you may be stuck while coupling or uncoupling your trailer. When that happens, the first step is to check the manufacturer's handbook for advice.

9. The correct answer is: (D). None of the above.

When checking the lower part of the fifth wheel, examine the locking jaws, the release arm and the lubrication condition. Ensure there are no spaces between the lower and upper parts.

10. The correct answer is: (B). Trailer frame.

The glide plate should be mounted on the trailer frame. If there is an issue with the mounting, such as damaged or missing parts, this is a serious problem.

11. The correct answer is: (A). To avoid hitting each other during turns.

Always check the distance between the tractor frame and the fifth wheel to ensure that these two parts are not hitting each other during turns. When they are in constant contact, they may cause severe damage that can impact how the vehicle handles.

12. The correct answer is: (C). Fully raised.

The landing gear must be fully raised to enable it to function at maximum capacity. If it is not raised or is only partially raised, something has gone amiss and the landing gear may malfunction.

13. The correct answer is: (D). Both A and B.

Another name for the tractor air supply control is trailer emergency valve. It is also known as a tractor protection valve control. When pushed in, the vehicle supplies the tractor with the air pressure and the valve cuts the air off when pulled out.

14. The correct answer is: (D). None of the above.

A comprehensive inspection of the trailer emergency brakes should include its parts, air pressure and its emergency position. Each plays a different role in the overall performance of the brake system.

15. The correct answer is: (A). Chock the wheels or apply the brakes.

Trailers need a lot of air for their brake system. Thus, it is imperative that you check your vehicle's air pressure regularly. Before you start, apply the brakes. If that doesn't work, chock the wheels. Always ensure the vehicle is completely stationary during the test.

16. The correct answer is: (A). Supplying air to the service line.

If you can supply the air successfully, it means the airflow mechanism is in good condition.

17. The correct answer is: (B). Trailer service brake.

A trailer service brake is needed for intermittent testing. You can use it to slow down or stop the vehicle.

18. The correct answer is: (D). Both A and C.

The trailer service brake needs the air pressure to function and its reliability is a guarantee against brake failure.

19. The correct answer is: (C). A tractor protection valve.

The air brake system must be fully protected from damage. Ensure the tractor protection valve gets the amount of air pressure it needs. Otherwise, the brake system may lose air pressure.

20. The correct answer is: (C). 20 to 45 psi.

Although the trailer needs a regular air supply, airflow to the trailer should be stopped when the air pressure drops to between 20 and 40 psi. Do this before you disconnect the line.

21. The correct answer is: (C). Air leaks.

Some landing gear is power-operated. Hence, it must be thoroughly checked for possible issues. Air leaks will deprive the landing gear of what it needs to operate correctly.

22. The correct answer is: (C). By lowering the second trailer's landing gear.

The landing gear is a retractable support that comes in handy to support and stabilize a trailer when its tractor has been removed. Thus, it supports the second trailer and keeps it off the dolly, thereby reducing its load considerably.

23. The correct answer is: (A). Through the emergency line shutoff.

If you want to check the second trailer for air, you can do that via the emergency line shutoff. Open it to check the trailer's air supply. If there is no air in the trailer, its brake will malfunction.

24. The correct answer is: (C). The trailer.

The crack-the-whip effect is most pronounced in the trailer part of a combination vehicle. This usually occurs when a trailer changes lanes quickly. This can result in a turnover.

25. The correct answer is: (D). No.

Some states do not permit triple trailers. Hence, you should be fully aware of your state's stance on triple trailers before you apply for a CDL that will permit you to operate such vehicles. Be aware that several states are relaxing their stance against triple trailers so the laws could eventually change.

Tanker Test 2 - 25 Questions

1. A space left on top of a tank during loading to accommodate expansion is called …
    a. An outage.
    b. A surge allowance.
    c. A bulkhead corrector.
    d. Expansion room.

2. A very important attribute of a liquid each driver should know prior to loading is …
    a. Its viscosity.
    b. Its capacity volume.
    c. Its expansion rate.
    d. Its boiling and freezing points.

3. What are baffles?
    a. Internal structures in a tank for storing extra liquids.
    b. Internal structures in a tank with some holes.
    c. Equipment that is specially designed for surge prevention.
    d. None of the above.

4. Baffles are necessary in tanks for …
    a. Bulkhead prevention.
    b. Surge prevention.
    c. Rollover prevention.
    d. Accident prevention.

5. What is the difference between baffles and smooth bore tanks?
    a. Baffles have internal partitions and smooth bore tanks don't.
    b. Smooth bore tanks have internal partitions but baffles don't.
    c. Smooth bore tanks are larger than baffles.
    d. Baffles are larger than smooth bore tanks.

6. Which of these tanks is used for transporting foods and food products?
    a. Smooth bore tanks.
    b. Baffles.
    c. Tanks with outage.
    d. Tanks with internal partitions.

7. When driving on wet roads, it is advisable to ...
    a. Double the stopping distance.
    b. Stop at your discretion.
    c. Reduce your speed considerably.
    d. Both A and C.

8. A safety precaution when entering a tunnel is to ...
    a. Blast your horn repeatedly.
    b. Accelerate a bit.
    c. Remove your sunglasses.
    d. All of the above.

9. Are tanker drivers legally obligated to obey speed limits when driving around corners?
    a. No.
    b. Yes.
    c. It's at their discretion.
    d. The law varies from state to state.

10. Who is responsible for cleaning up tanker spills?
    a. The Environmental Protection Agency.
    b. The Department of Transportation.
    c. The tanker driver.
    d. The Department of Road Safety.

11. One of the effects of quick steering is ...
    a. Rollover.
    b. Surging.
    c. Bulkheads.
    d. Brake failure.

12. When a tire slips on the road, this is known as ...
    a. Skidding.
    b. Overaccelerating.
    c. Sliding.
    d. Relative jackknifing.

13. The first corrective measure for skidding is to ...
    a. Release the brake after stopping.
    b. Release the brake midway through the skidding.
    c. Release the brake immediately.
    d. Release the brake at your convenience.

14. Which of the following areas should you check for leaks?
    a. Under the vehicle.
    b. The tires.
    c. The manhole covers.
    d. All of the above.

15. Covers and ports must have ...
    a. Gaskets.
    b. Manholes.
    c. Discharge ports.
    d. Hole sprays.

16. Some equipment all drivers must have includes ...
    a. Built-in fire extinguishers.
    b. Grounding or bonding cables.
    c. Vapor recovery kits.
    d. All of the above.

17. Electrical accessories are best connected with ...
    a. Electrical cables.
    b. Bonding or grounding cables.
    c. Electrical connectors.
    d. Electrical connecting devices.

18. Other parts of the vehicle you should inspect include all of the following except ...
    a. Hoses.
    b. Cut-off valves.
    c. Vents.
    d. None of the above.

19. The Tanker Endorsement Knowledge Test costs ...
    a. Between $10 and $50.
    b. $50.
    c. $100.
    d. $80.

20. When applying brakes, the pressure should be ...
    a. Increasing.
    b. Decreasing.
    c. Steady.
    d. Fluctuating.

21. It is advisable to ... when driving through a curve.
    a. Slow down.
    b. Accelerate significantly.
    c. Accelerate slightly.
    d. Slow down a little and increase speed.

22. All of the following can cause skidding in tankers except:
    a. Quick steering.
    b. Overaccelerating.
    c. Excessive braking.
    d. Checking the mirror for incoming vehicles.

23. A complete guide for tanker inspection can be found in/on ...
    a. YouTube.
    b. Google.
    c. Bing.
    d. The manufacturer's manual.

24. A vapor recovery kit is important ...
    a. To keep the vehicle clean.
    b. To reduce pollution.
    c. To ensure the vapor is free of contaminants.
    d. All of the above.

25. All drivers must always carry ...
    a. Personal Protection Equipment.
    b. Personal Protective Equipment.
    c. Personal Vehicle Protective Equipment.
    d. Personal Vehicle Protection Equipment.

Tanker Test 2 Answers

1. The correct answer is: (A). Outage.

A space left on the top of a tank during loading to accommodate expansion is known as an outage. The allowance helps to prevent dangerous spillage due to the expansion of a tanker's contents.

2. The correct answer is: (C). Its expansion rate.

A very important attribute of a liquid each driver must know and take into consideration is its expansion rate. This enables the driver to know the appropriate space to leave for the liquid to expand without constituting a nuisance during transportation.

3. The correct answer is: (B). They are internal structures in a tank with some holes.

Although baffles are somewhat similar to bulkheads, they are nothing but internal structures and don't actually serve as dividers for tanks as bulkheads do.

4. The correct answer is: (B). Surge prevention.

Surge arises as a result of the impact of the liquid on the tank during transportation. The holes in baffles make them ideal for preventing surge that may occur when transporting liquids.

5. The correct answer is: (A). Baffles have internal partitions and smooth bore tanks don't.

While baffles have internal partitions that make them great for surge prevention, smooth bores don't. Thus, they serve different purposes from each other.

6. The correct answer is: (A). Smooth bore tanks.

The smooth bore tanks' design makes them ideal for transporting foods and food products. Thus, they are used for hauling fruit juice, milk, drinking water, wine, etc. Baffles can't serve the same purpose due to their different design.

7. The correct answer is: (D). Both A and C.

Driving on wet roads can be challenging. The absence of friction between the roads and tires makes the vehicle more prone to skidding, rollover and other accidents. Thus, when driving on wet roads, it is advisable that you increase your stopping distance as well as reduce your speed.

8. The correct answer is: (C). Remove your sunglasses.

When entering a tunnel, remove any sunglasses to enhance your vision in the dark. You should also be prepared for a gush of air that will meet you at the exit.

9. The correct answer is: (A). No.

When approaching a tunnel, you will likely see posted speed limits. These are only intended for smaller cars. Safe driving is your priority, not a specific speed limit. Make sure you drive slowly in a tunnel, regardless of whether the speed limit is higher.

10. The correct answer is: (C). The tanker driver.

If you accidentally spill your tanker's contents on the road, you are personally and legally responsible for cleaning up the mess.

11. The correct answer is: (A). Rollover.

Rollover occurs when the vehicle can't keep up with the steering speed. An effective preventive measure is to steer the vehicle gently to make it easier for the vehicle to respond accordingly.

12. The correct answer is: (A). Skidding.

Skidding occurs when a tire loses traction on the road. This can cause terrible accidents.

13. The correct answer is: (C). Release the brake immediately.

You may be inclined to keep the pressure on the brakes with the hope of stopping the vehicle during a skid. However, that is counterproductive. A more efficient solution is to release the brakes immediately. Then, try to control the vehicle as much as you can.

14. The correct answer is: (D). All of the above.

A leak in your vehicle can make driving difficult, if not dangerous. Thus, when inspecting your vehicle, check for leaks everywhere. Check under the vehicle for signs of leaking fluid. Check the tires as well. Don't leave anything unchecked.

15. The correct answer is: (A). Gaskets.

Ports and covers must always have gaskets. Otherwise, severe damage can occur to a vehicle. Ensure your inspection includes checking to make sure these gaskets are in place and undamaged.

16. The correct answer is: (D). All of the above.

A tanker driver who takes safety seriously should have some special purpose equipment that can guarantee his/her safety and that of the vehicle. These pieces of equipment include grounding or bonding cables, built-in fire extinguishers and vapor recovery kits, among others. They will come in handy during emergencies.

17. The correct answer is: (B). Bonding or grounding cables.

Electrical accessories are best connected to the vehicle's chassis with bonding or grounding cables. This prevents these accessories from getting dangerously near the engine and/or making unnecessary contacts that can trigger a serious reaction, especially when live cables come in contact with iron or anything else.

18. The correct answer is: (D). None of the above.

Apart from checking under the vehicle for leaks, you should check for other damaged or missing parts as well. This implies that your check should include the cut-off valves, hoses, vents, etc.

19. The correct answer is: (A). Between $10 and $50.

The Tanker Endorsement Knowledge Test is a special endorsement test for potential tanker drivers. The test will cost you between $10 and $50, depending on your state of residence.

20. The correct answer is: (C). Steady.

When you are applying the brakes, keep the pressure steady. This enables you to control the vehicle with ease and avoid abrupt braking that can cause a wide range of problems such as skidding and rollover.

21. The correct answer is: (c). Accelerate slightly.

It is advisable that you take some extra precautions when navigating bends. This is to ensure that you maintain the right speed for safety's sake.

22. The correct answer is: (D). Checking the mirror for incoming vehicles.

Skidding can be caused in tankers by an array of factors. The most prominent of these are overaccelerating, quick steering and excessive braking.

23. The correct answer is: (D). Manufacturer's manual.

Although Google and YouTube may offer some valuable tips, the most reliable source of information pertaining to your vehicle's maintenance is the manufacturer's manual.

24. The correct answer is: (B). To reduce pollution.

Vapor recovery kits are used for recovering gasoline vapors and preventing them from escaping into the atmosphere. The goal is to reduce both pollution and potentially explosive fumes. As a safety precaution, it is advisable that you have this kit in your vehicle to handle emergencies.

25. The correct answer is: (B). Personal Protective Equipment.

Personal Protective Equipment such as eye protection, gloves and hard hats can lessen your exposure to deadly hazards. Always include these pieces of equipment in your tool box because you don't know when you'll need them.

Passenger Transport Test 2 - 25 Questions

1. An inspection under the vehicle should include:
    a. The driveshaft.
    b. The frame.
    c. The exhaust system.
    d. All of the above.

2. What is the appropriate speed for testing the service brake?
    a. 5 miles/hour.
    b. 4 miles/hour.
    c. 10 miles/hour.
    d. 20 miles/hour.

3. Are stickers appropriate on the windshield?
    a. Yes.
    b. No.
    c. It depends on where a sticker is located.
    d. It's up to a driver's discretion.

4. What are spare breakers or fuses used for?
    a. They are used for preventing damage to the fuses or breakers.
    b. They are used to replace blown fuses or breakers.
    c. They are used to prevent leaks.
    d. None of the above.

5. A good fire extinguisher must be ... and ...
    a. Partially charged and mounted.
    b. Mounted and fully charged.
    c. Red and fully charged.
    d. Partially charged and lightweight.

6. Triangles must be ...
    a. Blue and reflective.
    b. Red and opaque.
    c. Red and reflective.
    d. Green and reflective.

7. The aisle of a passenger vehicle must always be ...
    a. Clear and encourage free traffic flow.
    b. Allow extra space for physically challenged passengers.
    c. Be used at the driver's discretion.
    d. All of the above.

8. What are No-Zone areas?
    a. Parts of the road closed to heavy vehicles.
    b. Parts of the road closed to passenger buses.
    c. Blind spots with the potential for triggering crashes.
    d. Parts of the road where you can't pick up or drop off passengers.

9. Driving slowly is required when driving near ...
    a. Work areas and gas stations.
    b. No-Zone areas and gas stations.
    c. Work areas and No-Zone areas.
    d. Closed buildings and gas stations.

10. Crashes are more frequent ... on construction sites.
    a. Later in the day.
    b. At night.
    c. During the day.
    d. In the afternoon.

11. Two-thirds of traffic fatalities across the United States are caused by ...
    a. Driving under the influence of drugs or alcohol.
    b. Defensive driving.
    c. Aggressive driving.
    d. A and C.

12. ... and ... are two major characteristics of defensive driving.
    a. Keeping a safe distance between vehicles and maintaining a safe speed.
    b. Preventing other motors from overtaking you and blasting the horn.
    c. Driving on the right side of the road and playing loud music.
    d. Driving with the right license and endorsement.

13. ...is/are arguably one of the most important safety precautions for drivers.
    a. Regular and thorough inspections.
    b. Knowing how to drive on slippery roads.
    c. Fastening seat belts while driving.
    d. Applying the brakes at regular intervals.

14. Passenger buses are allowed to carry what class of ammunition?
    a. Special military ammunition
    b. Ordinary ammunition.
    c. Made in Korea ammunition
    d. Small-arms ammunition

15. Leaving baggage in the doorway can lead to ... and ...
    a. Obstruction and theft of the baggage.
    b. Obstruction and damage to the baggage.
    c. Damage to the doorway and the baggage.
    d. A and C.

16. Passenger vehicles cannot carry any of the following except:
    a. Class 6 poison.
    b. Division 2.3 poison gas.
    c. Radioactive materials in spaces meant for passengers.
    d. None of the above.

17. A passenger vehicle can transport all of the following except:
    a. Emergency hospital supplies.
    b. ORM-D.
    c. Small arms ammunition.
    d. Class 6 poison.

18. Under what conditions can a passenger vehicle transport animals?
    a. If they are owned by the driver and are being taken to a vet.
    b. If they are homeless and need serious medical attention.
    c. If they are for certified service or serve as guides.
    d. If they are hit by a hit-and-run driver and need urgent medical assistance.

19. A charter bus driver should only allow passengers in the vehicle ...
    a. When embarking on a trip.
    b. As soon as they arrive.
    c. 30 minutes before the trip.
    d. As determined by the driver.

20. What are the three triangles?
    a. A set of triangles with three different colors.
    b. A set of triangles you can put beside the road as a warning signal to other drivers of a crash ahead.
    c. Equal-sized triangles used in construction sites and passenger buses.
    d. A special type of triangle that serves different purposes in a vehicle.

21. What is a driveshaft?
    a. Another name for the gear.
    b. A device used for connecting the components of a drive train in a large vehicle.
    c. A special component specifically designed for passenger vehicles.
    d. A special driver for some components of the passenger bus.

22. The following are signs of a faulty driveshaft:
    a. Intense vibration underneath the vehicle.
    b. Shuddering while accelerating.
    c. Turning problems.
    d. All of the above.

23. A common problem you should look out for in a vehicle's frame is ...
    a. Cracks and loose bolts.
    b. Loose bolts and improper lubrication.
    c. Friction and cracks.
    d. Friction and loose bolts.

24. Abnormal noise in a driveshaft is caused by ...
    a. Improper lubrication.
    b. Failed or worn-out supporting bushings or bearings.
    c. Cracks or holes in the driveshaft.
    d. A deteriorating shaft handler.

25. These are all common problems in driveshafts except ...
    a. Shuddering during acceleration.
    b. Turning problems.
    c. Too much noise in the driveshaft.
    d. None of the above.

Passenger Transport Test 2 Answers

1. The correct answer is: (D). All of the above.

While checking under your vehicle, you should pay attention to several parts that include its frame, the exhaust system and the driveshaft. These parts play different roles in the vehicle and when any of them is faulty, it will have a huge impact on the vehicle's performance.

2. The correct answer is: (A). 5 miles/hour.

5 miles per hour is the most appropriate speed for testing the efficiency of the service brake. At that speed, it is easier to identify potential problems in the brake system as well as to gain insight into the overall efficiency of the system.

3. The correct answer is: (C). It depends on where a sticker is located.

A small sticker in the corner of the windshield where it doesn't obstruct the driver's view is harmless. The same can't be said of a large sticker that covers a significant portion of the driver's side, making it difficult for the driver to see clearly.

4. The correct answer is: (B). They are used to replace blown fuses or breakers.

Spare fuses or breakers are important vehicle accessories. They can blow out suddenly and that may pose a problem to the vehicle's electrical system.

5. The correct answer is: (B). Mounted and fully charged.

A fire extinguisher is of no use if it is not fully charged. Thus, you must ensure that your fire extinguisher is always fully charged and properly mounted where you can gain easy access to it during emergencies.

6. The correct answer is: (C). Red and reflective.

The red triangles are important safety equipment all drivers must have in their vehicles. They are used to warn drivers of a crash or accident ahead. For better visibility, especially at night, they must be red and reflective.

7. The correct answer is: (A). Clear and encourage free traffic flow.

The aisle is designed for free traffic flow, making movement easy for the passengers. Thus, it is imperative that aisles remain clear of obstructions.

8. The correct answer is: (C). Blind spots with the potential for triggering crashes.

No-Zones are blind spots along your driving route that may cause crashes or accidents if not properly identified and avoided. Running into a blind spot may cause a crash or accident that may damage the vehicle or vehicles, cause serious injuries, or loss of life.

9. The correct answer is: (C). Work areas and No-Zone areas.

Accidents can occur in work areas and No-Zone areas due to careless driving or excessive speeding. An effective preventive measure is to drive slowly while approaching such areas as well as when driving through them.

10. The correct answer is: (C). During the day.

While many drivers may be of the opinion that crashes are more frequent at night due to poor visibility, reports show that the reverse is the case because the frequency of road crashes during the day is higher.

11. The correct answer is: (C). Aggressive driving.

Some two-thirds of traffic casualties across the United States are caused by aggressive driving. This highlights the importance of driving defensively rather than aggressively.

12. The correct answer is: (A). Keeping a safe distance between vehicles and maintaining a safe speed.

Two of the major causes of road crashes and accidents are excessive speeding and driving too close to the vehicle in front. Many people drive too fast and leave little space to escape from danger.

13. The correct answer is: (C). Fastening your seat belt while driving.

Fastening your seat belt is arguably one of the most important safety precautions you can take while driving. The seat belt will hold you back during a crash, reducing the possibility of hitting the windshield with your head or hitting your chest on the steering wheel.

14. The correct answer is: (D). Small-arms ammunition.

While passenger buses are not designed for transporting ammunition, there are some exceptions. You can legally transport small arms ammunition that is clearly labeled ORM-D.

15. The correct answer is: (B). Obstruction of the doorway and damage to the baggage.

Leaving baggage in the doorway creates an obstruction to traffic. During emergencies or a stampede, the baggage may be destroyed completely or damaged beyond repair. Either of these situations can be avoided by keeping the doorway clear.

16. The correct answer is: (D). None of the above.

While passenger vehicles are allowed to carry some ammunition, drugs and emergency hospital supplies, under no condition are they permitted to carry division 2.3 poison gas, Class 6 poison or radioactive materials in spaces meant for human passengers. Failure to abide by these rules may result in severe penalties.

17. The correct answer is: (D). Liquid Class 6 poison.

You can transport ORM-D, emergency hospital supplies and small arms ammunition with your passenger vehicle. However, you are not licensed to transport Liquid Class 6 poisons such as phenol, clinical waste and some pesticides.

18. The correct answer is: (C). If they are for certified service or serve as guides.

Dogs and other animals are not allowed on a passenger vehicle. However, dogs can be allowed if they serve as guides for a physically challenged passenger or if they are certified service animals.

19. The correct answer is: (A). Embarking on a trip.

If you drive a charter vehicle, don't allow passengers to board your vehicle except when you are beginning a trip. This is to prevent vandalism to the vehicle and theft of passengers' baggage.

20. The correct answer is: (B). A set of triangles you can put beside the road as a warning signal to other drivers of a crash ahead.

A safety precaution for all drivers is to notify other road users of potential dangers. One way of doing this is to put three triangles beside the road to warn drivers of a crash or other danger ahead so that they can take necessary precautions.

21. The correct answer is: (B). A device used for connecting components of a drive train in a large vehicle.

A driveshaft, otherwise known as a tailshaft or propeller shaft, is a device used for connecting the components of a drive train in a large vehicle such as a passenger bus. When the shaft is faulty or damaged, it loses its connecting power and that may be disastrous.

22. The correct answer is: (D). All of the above.

It is very easy to detect a faulty driveshaft. The vehicle will shudder while accelerating, vibrate intensely in the undercarriage and/or be challenging to turn.

23. The correct answer is: (A). Cracks and loose bolts.

Loose bolts and cracks can cause a vehicle's frame to lose shape, raising the potential for an accident.

24. The correct answer is: (B). Failed or worn-out supporting bushings or bearings.

When the supportive bearing or bushing for the driveshaft U-joints or the driveshaft itself is failing, the result is usually clunking, rattling, squeaking or scraping.

25. The correct answer is: (D). None of the above.

Some common problems you may detect in your driveshaft include turning problems, shuddering during acceleration and excessive noise.

School Bus Test 2 - 25 Questions

1. The first step towards handling an emergency is ...
    a. Recognizing the problem.
    b. Seeking help.
    c. Fixing the problem.
    d. Shifting the blame on other road users.

2. What factor must you first consider when determining whether or not to evacuate students?
    a. Are they in greater danger if they remain on the school bus?
    b. How will their parents respond to the issue?
    c. What is the most appropriate time to notify the relevant authorities?
    d. What is the best place to move the students?

3. Under what conditions is evacuation mandatory?
    a. Higher possibility of accident and a threat of fire.
    b. If the bus changes position or hazardous materials spills around or on the bus.
    c. None of the above.
    d. All of the above.

4. When planning ahead for emergencies that may require student evacuation, you need the assistance of ... and ...
    a. Tall and agile students.
    b. Responsible and older students.
    c. Tall and older students.
    d. Responsible and final year students.

5. It's important to ... prior to an evacuation.
    a. Explain the evacuation procedures to the students.
    b. Take a roll call of the students.
    c. Organize students according to their needs.
    d. Call the relevant authorities.

6. When students are at risk from spilled hazardous materials ...
    a. Lead them downwind of the bus.
    b. Keep them in the vehicle with the windows and doors closed and locked.
    c. Lead them upwind of the bus.
    d. Reassure them of their safety.

7. When an emergency happens close to railroad tracks, you must ...
    a. Lead the students towards the railroad tracks for assistance.
    b. Lead the students away from the tracks.
    c. Lead the students away from the direction of oncoming trains.
    d. Call officials for assistance.

8. How do you secure a vehicle during emergencies?
    a. Shut the engine off and place the vehicle in neutral.
    b. Leave the ignition key in and activate the hazard lights.
    c. Keep the engine running and place the three triangles beside the vehicle.
    d. All of the above.

9. Which of these classes of students shouldn't be evacuated immediately?
    a. Older students.
    b. Students with head or neck injuries.
    c. Ill students.
    d. Foreign students.

10. You can ask all of the following people for assistance except:
    a. Passing motorists.
    b. Passing pedestrians.
    c. Responsible students.
    d. None of the above.

11. As a school bus driver, your knowledge should include:
    a. Accident prevention.
    b. Accident management.
    c. Accident prevention and management.
    d. Accident analysis, prevention and management.

12. You shouldn't release the students to any of the following people except:
    a. Parents.
    b. Neighbors.
    c. Other family members.
    d. None of the above.

13. The student evacuation process should begin with ...
    a. A call to the bus dispatch.
    b. A call to the emergency team.
    c. A visit to the nearby hospital.
    d. A call to your supervisor or the school authorities.

14. Some evacuation options you can choose from include:
    a. Roof hatch.
    b. Side doors.
    c. Rear and front door.
    d. All of the above.

15. Steer clear of the bus until it is declared fit for use by ...
    a. The police and accident management team.
    b. Bus dispatch and the relevant authorities.
    c. Bus dispatch and road safety management team.
    d. School authorities and the police.

16. When emergencies are caused by inclement weather, it is best to ...
    a. Keep the students in the vehicle until the weather improves.
    b. Keep the students in the vehicle until a rescue team arrives.
    c. Evacuate the students to a safe assembly area.
    d. Evacuate the student to a larger vehicle for immediate transportation to their destination.

17. What is a school lockdown?
    a. This refers to locking up a school during the holidays.
    b. This refers to a school closure triggered by power failure.
    c. This refers to the act of barring people from exiting or entering a school until further notice.
    d. None of the above.

18. Some common factors that can trigger a lockdown include all of the following except:
    a. Natural disasters.
    b. Police activity in the neighborhood.
    c. Medical emergencies.
    d. All of the above.

19. There are ... types of lockdown.
    a. Four.
    b. Three.
    c. Ten.
    d. Two.

20. Medical emergencies, weather-related emergencies and traffic jams are typical examples of a ...
    a. Code Black Lockdown.
    b. Code Yellow Lockdown.
    c. Code Red Lockdown.
    d. Code Green Lockdown.

21. Gunshots, a hostage situation and the presence of a dangerous person in or around the school are some typical examples of a ...
    a. Code Black Lockdown.
    b. Code Yellow Lockdown.
    c. Code Red Lockdown.
    d. Code Green Lockdown.

22. What is a shelter-in-place?
    a. This occurs when the school bus is contaminated with hazardous materials.
    b. It is a situation that may arise when the school environment is contaminated with hazardous materials.
    c. It refers to a location where students can be kept safe during a lockdown.
    d. It is a place for cleaning the school bus when contaminated with hazardous materials.

23. What should you do when your vehicle develops mechanical trouble?
    a. Drive it to a safe place before stopping.
    b. Secure it and activate the four-way flashers.
    c. All of the above.
    d. None of the above.

24. The Antilock Brake System that is designed to minimize skidding in school buses is ...
    a. Electronic controller.
    b. Wheel speed sensors.
    c. Modulators.
    d. A and B.

25. How many times are you allowed to retake the test per permit?
    a. Three times.
    b. Five times.
    c. Ten times.
    d. Two times.

School Bus Test 2 Answers

1. The correct answer is: (A). Recognizing the problem.

When you are faced with an emergency situation, recognizing the problem is the first step towards finding a solution. When you identify the source of the emergency, you are better equipped to fix it.

2. The correct answer is: (A). Are they at risk of exposure to greater danger if they remain in the school bus?

When contemplating whether to evacuate the students during an emergency or not, one of the most important factors you should consider is whether students are safer in or out of the school bus.

3. The correct answer is: (D). All of the above.

While you may be considering whether evacuation is necessary or if there are better alternatives, some situations demand immediate evacuation. This includes if the bus changes positions or hazardous materials spill on or around it. Evacuation is also necessary if there is a threat of fire or accident.

4. The correct answer is: (B). Responsible and older students.

When planning ahead for emergencies that may demand student evacuation, you need the assistance of responsible and older students. You can delegate some responsibilities such as leading the students to a safe place while you handle other important tasks to make the evacuation faster.

5. The correct answer is: (A). Explaining the evacuation procedures to the students.

Prior to the evacuation, it is imperative that you explain the evacuation process to the students. This will help ease their fears.

6. The correct answer is: (C). Lead them upwind of the bus.

When students are at risk of exposure to spilled hazardous materials, leading them upwind of the bus is one way to help keep them safe.

7. The correct answer is: (B). Lead the students away from the tracks.

When you are faced with an emergency situation very close to railroad tracks, you must lead the students away from the tracks. Move them in the direction of oncoming trains where you have better chances of getting the needed assistance as soon as possible.

8. The correct answer is: (A). Shut the engine off and place the vehicle in neutral.

You shouldn't overlook the importance of securing your vehicle in an emergency. Secure your vehicle by placing the vehicle in neutral. Then set the parking brakes and shut the engine off. Remove the ignition key and activate the hazard lights.

9. The correct answer is: (B). Students with head or neck injuries.

Don't evacuate students with head or neck injuries until professional medical personnel are on the ground to assist.

10. The correct answer is: (D). None of the above.

When in danger or during emergencies, don't hesitate to ask passing motorists, pedestrians and responsible students for assistance. With their assistance, you can easily manage the crisis until a professional rescue team or other professionals are on the ground to offer professional assistance.

11. The correct answer is: (B). Accident management.

As a school bus driver, you should have a wide range of knowledge including accident management skills. Such skills will come in handy during emergencies such as crashes. This enables you to take care of yourself and your students before help arrives.

12. The correct answer is: (D). None of the above.

You shouldn't release the students to the neighbors, parents or other family members without being documented and attended to by medical professionals. This is to ensure that the students receive the best medical attention before they are handed over to their respective families. The school authorities have a say too.

13. The correct answer is: (D). A call to your supervisor or the school authorities.

If it is mandatory that you evacuate the students, call the school authorities and your supervisors too. They should be aware of each step you take. The school authorities should be able to account for their students as well. They may also send help your way.

14. The correct answer is: (D). All of the above.

Side doors, the roof hatch, rear door and front door are some exits you can use for the evacuation. Choose the safest and easiest of the available options.

15. The correct answer is: (B). Bus dispatch and the relevant authorities.

If you are ever in danger, steer clear of the bus. Wait for the relevant authorities or bus dispatch to declare it fit for use. In the meantime, do everything within your power to ensure that your passengers are kept safe outside the vehicle.

16. The correct answer is: (C). Evacuate the students to a safe assembly area.

Sometimes, the emergency situation may be caused by inclement weather that may affect visibility and make driving too risky. In that event, evacuate the students to a safe assembly area until the weather improves and driving is safer. Keeping the students in the vehicle may put your life and theirs at risk.

17. The correct answer is: (C). It refers to the act of barring people from exiting or entering a school until further notice in response to a potential danger within the school environment.

A school lockdown refers to the act of barring people from exiting or entering a school until further notice. A school may decide on a lockdown in the face of danger that may include things such as riots, shootings, internal crises, etc.

18. The correct answer is: (D). All of the above.

Apart from the potential causes of lockdown mentioned above, other common factors that can trigger a lockdown include police activity in the neighborhood, medical emergencies and natural disasters. The lockdown is a preventive measure against the potential threat and ensures the safety and security of the school, staff and students.

19. The correct answer is: (B). There are three types of lockdown.

There are three types of lockdown: Code Yellow, Code Green and Code Red. Each lockdown type is unique and is triggered by different forms of threats.

20. The correct answer is: (B). Code Yellow.

Medical emergencies, weather-related emergencies and traffic jams are some typical examples of situations that may trigger a Code Yellow. Although it signifies that danger isn't imminent within the school premises, all staff and students are still required to stay in the building.

21. The correct answer is: (C). Code Red.

Gunshots, a hostage situation and the presence of a dangerous person in or around the school are some situations that can trigger a Code Red. This situation may endanger everyone on the school premises. Thus, the students should be kept out of sight and this may require taking them to a safe place.

22. The correct answer is: (A). This occurs when the school bus is contaminated with hazardous materials.

A shelter-in-place situation may arise when the environment where the school bus is at a point in time is contaminated with hazardous materials that may endanger the lives of the passengers on the bus. You may either need to drive the vehicle away from the contaminated environment or seal off the bus completely.

23. The correct answer is: (C). All of the above.

Your vehicle may develop mechanical problems when least expected. To ensure the vehicle's safety as well as that of your passengers, it is advisable to drive to a safe place before stopping the vehicle. Then, secure the vehicle and activate the four-way flashers.

24. The correct answer is: (A). Electronic controller.

The electronic controller in the Antilock Brake System is designed to minimize skidding in school buses while helping the driver to maintain steering control even in extremely difficult braking conditions. It uses the wheel speed sensors to analyze the speed in all the vehicle's wheels and compare them.

25. The correct answer is (A). Three times per permit.

You can retake the test within a couple of days or at your convenience. If you fail the first retake, you can only take the test again after waiting for at least 90 days to improve your knowledge and skills. Each permit allows you to retake the test three times.

Conclusion

If you are seeking a career in the trucking industry, it is imperative that you have the right type of license and endorsement.

Familiarize yourself with the different Commercial Driver's Licenses discussed in this book alongside their endorsements and choose the most appropriate for you.

Look at the requirements and see whether you meet them or not. If you do, good luck! Take the required tests, both practical and theoretical, to obtain your license.

Understand the basic precautionary measures and study the proven tips that will ensure safety on the road. Don't forget the importance of routine vehicle inspection. Implementing these suggestions will make it easier to get licensed and pursue your career.

Made in the USA
Columbia, SC
06 May 2021